A veteran teacher shares wisdom
she learned from her students.

I'M JUST A KID, YOU KNOW!

Norma K. Salway

Norma K. Salway

Library of Congress Catalog Card No.: 2013949058

Salway, Norma K.
I'm Just a Kid, You Know

Norma K. Salway
p. 176
1. Education : Elementary
2. Education : Teaching Methods & Materials - General.
3. Education : Students & Student Life
I. Title.

Softcover: 978-1-934949-71-9
Kindle: 978-1-934949-73-3
Smashwords: 978-1-934949-80-1

JWB
Just Write Books
www.jstwrite.com
Topsham, ME 04086
Printed in the United States of America

Contents

Dedicated to the talented students of Crescent Park School who enriched my life forever. Thank you for your gifts of wisdom and joy that you bestowed upon me. I was proud to be your teacher.

All names have been changed
to protect the privacy of students and others.

Who dares to teach must never cease to learn.

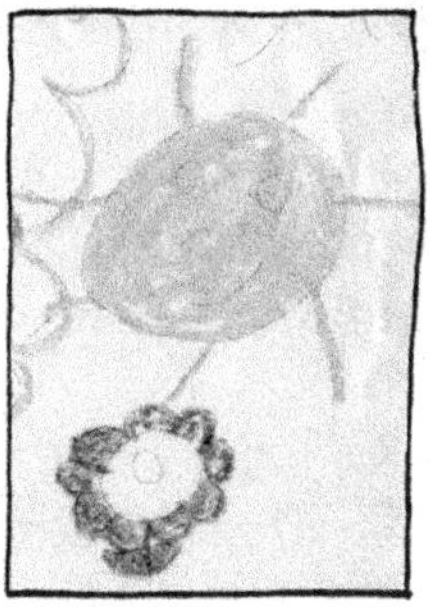

Chapter One
One Last Look

As I grasped the handle of the door to my first grade classroom, I stopped to gaze around the room, one last check to be sure everything was in order. This last minute self-imposed inspection was a ritual I'd performed for twenty-two years. The first glance was always toward my desk. I hate a cluttered desk: cluttered desk, cluttered mind. My brain always felt a little clearer with at least one open space on top of my desk. There could be piles on either side, but in the center there had to be no clutter. Plus, I didn't want any parent to walk by and notice that this teacher's desk was cluttered. They might think, cluttered desk, cluttered mind. Do I want HER teaching my child?

This day was different. It was June. This day was my last day of teaching. My last class of students had left at two-thirty. There would be no more first days of school. NO more glances around the room before I went home. Today, I retired. It was so quiet. Tomorrow would begin the difficult task of sorting through papers, files, boxes, folders, shelves and over-accumulation of teaching materials. Now, I found myself sorting through the emotions I was experiencing. I loved teaching. How can I be leaving a profession I cherished for so long?

"You'll know," a wise veteran teacher once cautioned me. "You'll know when it's time for you to leave."

I knew.

But, here I was with a lump in my throat and stacks of boxes to pack in the morning instead of packing away for another year. Here I was standing at the threshold of enormous changes in my life. Not easy for a creature of habit. Oh yes, I'll admit, change had not always come easily.

Teaching did provide me with the day-by-day routines I enjoyed. However, life in the classroom everyday was anything but routine. No two days were ever alike. Teeth do not fall out on schedule. Kids do not vomit when the basket is nearby. Tears do not flow on cue. One of the most important lessons I learned right away from the early days in a primary classroom is that any teacher's middle name quickly becomes "Flexible" with a capital F. And, if you can't be flexible, you will not survive.

Along with many other firsts, I learned that one has to be willing to grab those teachable moments and throw out the plan book. There will be days, actually many, when you wonder why you even have a plan book because of the "I" word—interruptions. Of course, plan books are mandatory. It's also mandatory in some districts to have precise curriculum standards in notation beside each entry validating the reason for that particular lesson.

Now, don't get me wrong. Interruptions do not always mean negative events. In fact, many teacher interruptions are "II," important interruptions. So, it's very important to write plans in pencil, just in case you have to make last minute changes. New teachers, you will.

Teaching in an elementary classroom prepares one for just about any crisis, because a crisis can happen any day of the week. It might be a minor crisis, or it might be a major one, but they will happen. What you need to know is no textbook is going to prepare you for it. But on the job training will. The crisis might involve blood from an unexpected nosebleed. It might involve a lock-down caused by a nearby bank robbery. It might involve a lost boot or yogurt spilled in a backpack. It might involve an upset parent or an upset administrator, or an upset student. It might be all on the same day. However, all involve your action, timing, and tact.

Early in life, I made a conscious decision to try to make a positive difference in the lives of children. In return, however, I discovered that those children made a lasting difference in my own life. Children look at the world in their own set of all-encompassing eyes. They view the details of our natural surroundings with introspective wonder, observing moments that busy adults miss in their scurried pace of everyday living.

Children gain delight from the simplest of objects. They find joy in discovering a pebble that resembles a human tooth or a noticing a cloud shaped like a giant pterodactyl.

"Look, there's a dinosaur up in the sky."

Children marvel at the sound of a grasshopper's song or peepers on a spring night. Children notice the crinkle in our brows and realize we're worried. They believe in miracles and assist doubting elders in their midst to believe, too. Children know how to express joy in a splendorous occasion or accomplishment of a task by gushing with bubbly enthusiasm and appreciation, shouting, "Ain't this just awesome?"

When was the last time you shouted, "Ain't this just awesome?"

Of course, inquisitive eyes and ears are often so intrigued and side-tracked by worldly distractions that they miss the important lesson being delivered at the moment of impact.

Some children are sensitive to the trials of the disadvantaged and share cries of pain at the sight of an injured creature at the side of the road while covering their eyes to shield their anguish. Kids marvel at the moon and think it's moving along with the car accompanying them on a night's journey. Children sense and read our emotions when we think we're hiding our feelings from the outside world.

"Are you sad about something?"

Children say what's on their minds and broaden our views with their daring questions.

"Why isn't it okay to pick our noses and put it in our mouths?" Come on, I know there are readers who did just that as a child and were told to stop.

"Are you pregnant? Your belly is sticking out."

Although it's important for us to grow up and out of the bad habits, we should revisit the pleasures and responses to the smaller wonders of everyday life and remember to shout out, "Ain't that just awesome?"

As I closed the door, I reached down into my inner emotions, shaking out the multitudes of feelings circling round and round. As I walked down the familiar hallway toward the front lobby, I carried with me many fond memories of life in the classroom and the lessons I learned about kids and life. Throughout this book I attempted to share the joys and sorrows, the fears and tears, the anxieties and frustrations, the laughter and insight of daily life while simultaneously confronted with meeting the needs of students under my wings of responsibility. I often felt like Mary Poppins and a mother duck rolled into one.

Don't be afraid to make a mistake.

Chapter Two
Assumptions

A younger colleague, however a veteran, seasoned teacher, walked into my classroom the day before my first day of teaching. She was at least ten years younger than I.

"I am here to give you a piece of advice about teaching," she announced with a chuckle, "and you'd better take heed to my warning."

Placing her arm around my shoulders, she looked me straight in the eye and spoke directly and distinctly, "Never, ever, assume anything when it pertains to kids and teaching. For if you do, the first three letters of that word 'assume' will get the better of the last three."

I stood there with my mouth open contemplating her words of wisdom, spelling the letters to myself. Let me see, the first three letters are "a-s-s." The last three letters are "u-m-e."

Laughing aloud she consoled me.

"Oh, you have a lot to learn. Beware. Assumptions can

quickly make asses of you and me."

I tried to follow this advice. However, more than once, I found myself a victim.

When I began my educational career I was fortunate to spend eight years working as a teacher's aide in a three-room elementary school in the middle of a small Maine village. During that initial year I also took my first college course ever. The terms "green horn," "novice," and "you've got a lot to learn" were commonly expressed to describe me. At the time, I had not considered a career in teaching. After all, I was twenty-nine years old, a wife, and mother of two school-aged children.

I was amazed at the daily demands on teachers and had no idea all the time spent on lesson preparation. Throughout those early years, I was overwhelmed with the demands required of those in the teaching profession. Those demands included mastering educational jargon that somehow I didn't learn from the parent's end and was too embarrassed to question at the time.

As a teen, wondering what career path to choose, I purposely stated that I would never be a teacher because that's what my oldest sister was studying to be. Being the independent person that I was, I stubbornly vowed that I would follow a totally different path. I would make my own career choice.

However, those years spent as an aide in that small school setting, provided the best teacher preparatory training anyone could ever experience. It gave me insight into the daily lives and profession of teachers and their students. I was not just a classroom teacher-helper there. My job description read more like a jack-of-all trades aide. Throughout the school day I was required to step into various roles.

First, I was the school secretary. My old wooden desk was located in a large hall opening between the boys' and the girls' one-seater bathrooms at the back of the aging school. There was even an old unused two-seater wooden outhouse-style bathroom connected to the boys' room. That brought a few chuckles to the state school inspector. Gripping his clipboard, he announced with a grin that it was the first time he'd had an opportunity to place a check mark next to the item, two-seater, on his official list. Beyond my desk was an entrance to the unheated storage room at the rear of the one hundred-year-old school.

For the first few years, I was required to report the daily attendance and lunch count to the office of a neighboring school a few miles further south on Route 26. Now this should be nothing unusual, except it definitely was. You see our phone system was part of the only remaining operating crank phone system in the entire United States.

In order to make a call, I had to first crank the phone one long crank to access the operator who was located in the next town.

"What number please?" The operator would ask.

"Six, one, ring two," I'd reply. Eventually, the friendly operator would recognize my voice and put me through automatically to the office of the Woodstock Elementary

School.

Another task of my job was performing outside playground duty every morning before school started and during the noon recess. One foggy fall morning, a little boy came running wide-eyed around the corner of the schoolhouse gasping while trying to get words out.

"There's someone sleeping behind the school. He's by the rocks. Who is it? Why is he sleeping behind the school?"

My feelings exactly. I took the young child's outstretched hand and directed him to show me this stranger.

I must admit I approached with caution and advised the children to stay back. I stood over the now awake gentleman. He was middle-aged with a beard, slightly reminiscent of Gulliver.

Can you imagine awakening to the sight of ten or so children staring at you with looks of wonderment?

The now wide-awake fellow was struggling to pull up his pants, step out of his sleeping bag, while coping to maintain balance, and attempting to explain his presence.

"I'm sorry to alarm you, ma'am. I thought I had found the backyard of a church. The night was so foggy I guess I couldn't tell. I didn't know this was a school. I'm hiking to New Hampshire."

I motioned for the animated students to follow me back around the schoolhouse to the front entrance so the guest could pack up his gear and vacate the playground.

After I rang the school's hand bell to announce it was time to go inside, I could hear the chorus of voices all trying to explain at once to their teachers about the man who had been sleeping on the playground behind the school.

Another morning, I received a call from the district nurse informing me that she would be bringing down a stack of letters to be sent home to parents. She further explained that the letter was an informational letter about pediculosis. I'm sure there was a long pause on the end of the line at this request. When the nurse arrived I explained my lack of knowledge of this new term. We laughed together at the strange but formal name for this often terrifying condition commonly known as lice.

There is nothing more embarrassing than encountering a word for which I didn't have a clue as to its meaning. I soon found myself learning a whole new vocabulary of educational jargon.

Administrators and teachers often, although not intentionally, use language and terms that are confusing for parents. However, I learned to ask and not assume.

There are gross motor skills versus fine motor skills. Now when I hear the word gross, I visualize slimy and green. However I soon learned that in the school community it means large muscles and small muscles as in the movements of our legs or in our fingers.

At the risk of revealing my lack of teacher training early in my career, I point out this confusion in support of parents. Too often, we toss out these words in parent–teacher conferences without considering that perhaps there is a communication gap.

Here is just a sampling of educational jargon parents will soon learn:

Anecdotal records, benchmark testing, behavior modification, auditory learner, kinesthetic, tactile, differential learning, extrinsic motivation, intrinsic motivation, manipulatives, rubrics, homogeneous grouping, heterogeneous grouping, trade books, IEP, NWEA. NCLB, OT, PT, ADD, ADHD, ESL, and on and on.

My advice is to go online to a search engine and type in the words "educational jargon for parents," and you'll be surprised at the information you will find. I've included a simple glossary at the back of the book.

Smile.

Smile, and gather as much knowledge about other professions as possible. Because, in the home and in the classroom, you need to be proficient in many areas of information, garner the skills from detective to dentist, from orchestra conductor to bloodhound, to mind reader; the combined traits of Mary Poppins and a mother duck will just not work.

Chapter Three
Literal Translations

Kids often interpret what we say literally.

Those blunders are enlightening for any first time parent and always surprise teachers.

They misinterpret what we say or don't hear what we said at all, even though we said it repeatedly. Do you follow? Kids often don't. Another lesson: repeat, repeat, repeat any information or directions.

And, most importantly teachers and parents: kids don't always hear it correctly. Beware!

"You never said to do that."

"I never heard you."

"But, that's what you told me to do."

A little girl once bent her head down and asked me if she had lice.

"What makes you think you have lice?"

"A boy on the bus tells kids that all the time."

To this remark, another pigged-tailed friend interjected,

"You know it's that green stuff that grows in your hair."

Bewildered, I responded, "I'm not sure what you're talking about."

As they left the room I overheard one student say to a nearby teacher, "Mrs. F, Ms. Salway doesn't know what lace is" as she inspected her clothes for frills.

Another time, a kindergarten child walked up to me near the bookcase and announced that her mom had recently given her "highlights."

"Oh, is it like the one on the shelf?" (Thinking it was the children's magazine by that name.)

"No. She gave me blond highlights."

During flu season there was a discussion outside the girls' bathroom about catching the flu.

"I think she caught it [the flu] between Bethel City and Albany."

"Oh, no, I think I've caught the diarrhea," a little girl wailed as she retreated into the bathroom.

Winter conditions in Maine often cause outside steps to ice over. On this particular January morning, the janitor asked if I would remind students that during recess time they should not play near the back fire door, as he had put down salt to help melt the ice. And also remind the students to never, ever put the salt into their mouths.

After I explained the safety concerns to the kindergarten, first and second grade students, a blond-haired boy in a knit cap and a puzzled look on his face, raised his hand.

"If we eat the salt, will WE MELT?"

I'm Just a Kid, You Know

As I was working one-on-one with a kindergarten student helping him to form the letters in his name, I instructed him to start by placing the pencil on the line. He did exactly what I asked him to do. He picked up the pencil and laid it down parallel to the line.

One of my favorite stories told by a veteran teacher was about misinterpretation and the consequences.

My dear colleague was serving outside playground duty when a little boy with hearing problems came up to her saying, "Boo-boo," while pointing to his finger.

"Oh, a boo-boo, I'll kiss it and make it better." She placed the little boy's smudged finger to her lips and kissed it.

An older child approached the smiling teacher shaking her head in disapproval.

"Mrs. C., you shouldn't have done that. He was trying to tell you that he had dog poo. He fell down on the playground and his hand plopped into a pile of dog poop."

I think the folks at the supermarket down the street must have heard the shriek of surprise.

As the class was getting ready for D.E.A.R. time (Drop Everything and Read), a little girl missing two front teeth asked me where her favorite book was located. I told her it was on the easel. A few minutes later she returned with a bewildered look, without the book, and whispered into my ear, "Where's the weasel?"

Oftentimes, we use terms freely without realizing that children don't understand common slang. Our school library had a new computer system installed to make the process of checking out books run more smoothly. When new books arrived with the new system, they contain bar codes that are scanned into a computer, replacing the outdated library card system. Our efficient librarian was also able to check ISBN numbers by scanning in the bar code.

One winter afternoon, my first grade students were waiting a turn to have their new books scanned and checked out by the librarian.

"What are you doing with that thing?" a child asked as the librarian scanned across the black lines at the bottom of the book with the small gray wand.

"The computer reads it. Then, spits it out," she replied, referring to the bar code.

With a puzzled look on his face, the young boy asked, "How does the computer do that—spit it out?"

Sometimes, we don't realize when we are teaching important content material that our information is not always being received as we intended.

While teaching a lesson on subtraction to first graders, I introduced them to the term for the answer, "remainder or difference." But, later, when reviewing, I used the term "left over."

I became confused and concerned when a bright little girl who seemed to understand the math concept began writing unusual answers. Where and how was she getting her answers, I questioned myself? I asked her to come up to my table for individual help, and I watched as she proceeded to subtract the bottom number (subtrahend) from the top larger number (minuend). However, the numerals she wrote down made no sense at all.

After close observation, I asked her to explain to me what she had learned and how she was getting her answers. She went on to tell me that what was left, pointing to the number farthest to the LEFT directionally, was the answer. Wow, I was dumbfounded. It taught me to be very careful about my teaching delivery. Some children pick up on everything. I had unknowingly used the term, "left over" and left her completely confused. She had taken the meaning literally, especially since we had also been working to strengthen the children's understanding of right and left.

Be aware of how misinformation can make its way unintentionally into the minds of developing children. Is it any wonder that teaching can be so challenging?

My elder sister, a retired teacher with over twenty-five years of experience told this story of the double meaning of words and how those misinterpretations often translate into humorous situations.

This fledgling teacher was lining up her second grade students preparing to go outside for morning recess. She proceeded to give a final reminder to the energetic group about appropriate behaviors before exiting the classroom. A few of the lively boys grabbed brightly colored playground balls to toss around.

"Remember to walk quietly, please."

"And boys, hang on to your balls."

And, in unison, all the little boys did just that.

A retired second grade teacher, now in her eighties, recalled one of her favorite teaching stories about an incident that happened many years ago. Her students were participating in a classroom art project when one student announced abruptly, "Teacher, I ain't got no blue."

Politely, she attempted to correct his English grammar and choice of words.

"I don't have any blue," she responded.

To this admonishment, the young boy was overheard saying to a classmate nearby, "Why the hell does she need a blue, she ain't even painting."

When my youngest granddaughter was eight, she started questioning me about what school was like when I was growing up. I began to relate some of the differences in schoolrooms then and now.

"Back when I was a kid in grammar school, we didn't have all the learning materials that you have today. We didn't have computers, games, math materials, and classroom libraries with shelves full of colorful interesting books."

With this explanation, she sat quietly, then turned to me with a serious look on her face and replied, "I didn't know there was a school to learn to be a grandma."

After engaging the class in a writing lesson before the beginning of journal writing time, I reminded students to be sure to begin every sentence with a capital letter and to place a period at the end. I also added a verbal reminder to students to be sure to check all their work before placing it in the "work done" basket. That evening while reading the journal entries, I noticed one journal entry had a checkmark placed above every letter in every word on the whole page.

The next morning, I asked the young writer why she had placed checkmarks above every letter.

"You told us to check all our work, so I did."

As a culminating event to highlight our grade-one unit "Then and Now," I invited the entire grade one students to my house on a field trip to spend the day participating in historical activities. One group sat at old school desks, another group washed clothes with a washboard and tub, another made butter and talked on vintage phones, some watched spinning, and others enjoyed a display of vintage hats and clothing. I showed students my parents' original ten-inch-tall cabinet television. I nonchalantly described how we used "rabbit ears" to assist with reception. Not realizing the affect of those words, a young lad's eyes opened wide. "Cool. You had a real bunny sitting on top of your TV?"

One of the memorable lessons I learned from a child about miscommunication occurred early in my career while working as a teacher's aide. As part of my job, I gave individual reading instruction to students under the direction of the Title I teacher. On this particular morning, I walked quietly into the second grade classroom to bring a little girl back into my area to receive extra help. Usually I would walk over to her desk and tap her on the shoulder so not to disturb the rest of the class. However, since we had been working together for several weeks, I decided to stand in the doorway, catch her eye, and motion for her to come, thinking it would be less distracting. I stood in the doorway, caught her eye, and all seemed well.

Her big, brown eyes looked directly into mine. She didn't move an inch. I motioned with my index finger for her to come to me. She looked me straight in the eyes and once again, did not budge. Two more times, I motioned for her to come to the door, but she ignored my gesture each time. Finally, I walked over to her, gently took her by the hand and guided her into my room.

As she sat down in the little wooden chair, I asked her why she didn't walk to the door when I motioned.

She looked up at me with those brown eyes wide open and said, "It's not nice to stick up your middle finger."

I nearly fell out of my chair from hearing her response.

"You thought I was sticking up my middle finger at you?" I asked.

"Yes. That's not nice," she repeated with a slight tone of annoyance.

After giving her a sincere clarification lesson in finger names and reassuring her of the meaning of motioning with an index finger, we laughed together about the mistake.

I assumed she knew what I meant when I gestured with my finger. I was wrong.

Inside the whirlwind of thoughts and ideas growing in

the minds of little children, there often lies confusion and misconceptions concerning the events that fashioned those beliefs. As adults, we would be wise to remember that children do not process information exactly as we do.

Throw your uglies into the garbage.

Chapter Four
Nobody's Perfect

"You would never realize it now, but growing up I was a very shy child."

Many times I reassured worried parents with these words when they expressed concerns about their overly shy child. My birth order might have been a contributing factor since I was born second from the oldest, a middle child, one of four girls. But I just lacked self-confidence. It was perfection, I suspect. I thought I had to be perfect. If I opened my mouth, the wrong words might come out. Maybe it was because I fell out of the car when I was little. I leaned on the car door. It opened. I fell out. Luckily the car was only pulling out of our gravel driveway when the incident occurred. I was too young to remember it, but I always heard the details of the story. Actually, I'm sure my shyness had nothing to do with me falling out of a car, but it's a more interesting reason.

I had made a mistake. What if I hadn't leaned on that door? Remember, it was in the days before seatbelts.

Oh, perhaps, my shyness was due primarily to the fact that we lived in the country, on a dirt road, with the only neighbors a half a mile away. "Socially isolated," I think I once heard a teacher remark when I didn't want to say my name out loud. First of all, I didn't like my name. It was old-fashioned. Norma Jean. Ugh. I wanted a modern sounding name like my friends had like Dee-Dee, Judy, Darlene, Nancy, Betsy, Jackie, or Suzanne. Norma Jean was not the perfect name. I was once asked, "Why did your parents name you that?"

Many well-intentioned people tried to remedy my fixation with my lack-luster name by pointing out that Marilyn Monroe's real name was Norma Jean Baker. My response was, " If it was such a great name, then why did she change it to Marilyn Monroe?"

Then came the request to speak my name aloud.

I never say my name aloud. Other people say my name. My three sisters say my name. My parents say my name.

I was about four years old and I remember exactly where I was when I was asked to say my name aloud in the presence of a large amount of people. I froze with fear at having to do this seemingly easy task during a gathering circle at vacation bible school. Finally, after futile attempts to pry my name out of my mouth, my older sister was called into the big room where we were all standing in a circle.

"Her name is Norma and she is shy."

Now, why couldn't I do that? I knew then that I had a big problem.

As a first grader back in 1951, my teacher handed out math paper to every student, but she inadvertently skipped over me. Fearing I had made a mistake, I began to cry. The teacher could not have made a mistake, after all. A little boy sitting next to me, sensing my distress, raised his hand and told the teacher that I didn't have a piece of paper. I had a crush on that little guy for the longest time after that incident. He was my hero.

"Oh, Norma Jean, next time, just raise your hand to tell me," the teacher suggested apologetically.

Raise my hand and speak out, in front of the whole class. I don't think so. But, I wanted too. I wanted to be able to speak up, but the words would just not come out of my mouth. I repeated the words in my thoughts but I could not push them out. The words froze inside my mouth clumped together in the back of my throat, like a hairball. Except, I had word-balls.

Another time, when I was about seven or eight, I was returning from a visit to the house of a friend who lived in town. I sat next to her in the rear seat of her parents' car. My mother had reminded me to be sure to say, "thank you for the nice time," when I was dropped off back at our farmhouse.

I can't believe the anxiety I went throughout the entire five miles from her house to our farmhouse in the country.

Over and over to myself I repeated the words, "Thank, you Mrs. Howe. I had a nice time." I don't think I heard any of the conversation during that ride because I concentrated so much on the courage to get those words out.

Finally, we pulled into our driveway. My heart pounded as I slowly took a deep breath and pushed out the words in a barely audible soft voice. But, my long practiced speech actually came out of my mouth. Whew. I was so relieved. And, I was actually proud of myself.

It was awful to be burdened by such shyness.

Over the years, I gained more and more self-confidence and learned to speak in front of the class. It was not easy. Most of my report cards, even through high school, stated, "needs to contribute more during class discussions."

But, I was surprised to learn that the more I spoke, the easier it became.

Then there were the annual Christmas programs where students had to "speak a piece." Whenever I mention this term now, in conversation, I can immediately tell the age of the person who's in the room, if he or she understands the school tradition to which I referred.

"Oh, my word, I remember having to recite those poems back in the fifties. We had to memorize a short poem and stand up in front of all our parents at the school Christmas party and recite a poem by heart. Usually, we had to wear a hat or carry a prop that reflected the theme of the poem."

One of my treasured possessions is an old teacher's book of *Pieces and Plays*, published in 1916. In it are many short recitations with names of students penciled in beside the poems. Here is one with the names of several boys who had been assigned this particular piece, but in different years.

A Possibility
I've said "Please" all the last two weeks,
I've washed and combed my hair,
And run errands for all the folks
With never a minute to spare.
It's awfully hard before Christmas
To remember all these things;
Guess if it was any longer
That I'd be sprouting wings.
Winifred A. Hoag.

I never forgot how terribly shy I was. These memories, however, served me well during my years teaching. Every year on the first day of school, I reminded students that they would make mistakes and they would learn from those mistakes. Even I, their teacher, would probably make a few. I clarified that remark with the suggestion that we try our best, but mistakes do happen. As a teacher, I understood only too well the agony a child suffering from shyness would face. I did my best to help develop self-confidence in those students.

These shy students taught me something else. They usually were very well-behaved, and listened well. As a result, they were good academic students.

On the first day of school many years ago, first grade students walked eagerly into the classroom and looked for their name tag taped to the top of the desk before settling into their new seat. As I was explaining procedures and materials, I requested students to look inside their desks and take out their own colorful "workboxes." Inside those rectangular plastic boxes they would find their own box of new crayons, a couple of sharpened pencils, and a big pink squishy eraser that resembled a piece of bubble gum.

One little girl sitting close to the front of the room where I was standing was squirming around in her seat. Soon, classmates close to her started chatting. I said to her, "You didn't take out your workbox as I asked? How come?"

She gave me this puzzled look.

"I can't get into my desk."

"You can't get into your desk? Let's see, what is the problem?"

As I leaned down to examine the desk, I realized that when I pushed the desks into place, this one was turned the wrong way with the opening to the back. This caused the side facing her to be inaccessible. No wonder she couldn't retrieve her box. She couldn't get into her desk.

Students have a knack of saving the day and somehow can make the teacher look good when yes; the teacher has made a mistake.

One little girl quickly remarked, "See, you did make a mistake, Mrs. S., but it's okay."

I couldn't have planned a better lesson if I've done it

on purpose. I think some students thought I had actually turned the desk around on purpose to make a point.

Another time, I was giving instructions on using a glue bottle correctly. Why, you question? Why would you give a lesson in using a glue bottle? Every child knows how.

No, they don't.

It is a very important lesson to instruct students in the proper way to replace those glue bottle little orange caps. If tops are not screwed down tightly, we all know what happens. No glue comes out for the next person. Then, it never fails, right in the midst of reading group someone groans, "None of the glues work. I can't do my work."

Or, a self-reliant child decides to poke a new hole in the small orange cap by stabbing the point of scissors down through the top. However, she accidently stabs her finger which needs immediate attention. Get the point?

During one of my annual beginning-of-the-year group guidance lessons demonstrating "proper use of glue bottles," I stood at the front of the classroom where all could see. I grasped the bottle of glue upside down preparing to show the correct amount to use. As I proceeded to squeeze the bottle, the top suddenly popped off and glue came pouring out all down my hand and onto the startled student sitting directly beneath me.

Eighteen excited voices all rang out at once.

"Oh no, Mrs. S. You dumped glue all over David!"

Sure enough, I had indeed. A trail of sticky white glue drizzled down the child's arm, onto his shirt, and flowed over his desktop oozing toward the floor.

Again, a first grader came to my rescue. Even before I could get the words out, this little cherub spoke the words as if on cue, "Remember, Mrs. S., everybody makes mistakes, even you."

"And what did we all learn from this mistake?"

"Always screw the cap down." children shouted in unison.

Another teachable moment salvaged by the wise words from an observant, confident child. Another lesson well taught by accident.

Nobody is perfect. No child is perfect. No parent is perfect. No teacher is perfect.

But, that doesn't mean that we as parents and teachers make excuses for inappropriate actions and behaviors of our children. Discipline is at the core of parenting and teaching.

Perfection—no. Discipline—yes.

Chapter Five
Red Dots

I had a secret. I had this little secret since I was in first grade. Oh, this hidden matter was not about any horrible experience that happened. To many it was rather mundane, in fact. However, to me, it was more about coping when you're six. My secret had to do with the reliance on "red dots."

Tall, small-paned windows covered in frost filled one wall of the large classroom that overlooked the playground. The smell of wax crayons, oranges from recess snack, jars of paste, (I can't believe I sometimes ate that paste as a kid) and heat rising from the radiators, permeated the air. Thirty desks were pushed together in groups forming small islands of tables throughout the open spaces. A sand table stood in one corner in front of the blackboards. I sat in a small wooden chair at one of these groupings with boys and girls seated all around.

I discovered that I was not alone in liking the taste of

that wheat paste used to glue paper together. In conversations with many of my former classmates, they too admitted that they had often eaten paste. The school paste we used in the 1950s was made of flour and water, much like the consistency of wallpaper paste. It came in large white jars or in small reusable jars with little spreaders. One of my sisters who taught school for over twenty years told me that one year she had to hide the paste because she had two little boys who ate it as if it were peanut butter. I liked letting the paste dry on my hands and finger tips and then peeling it off. The downside to this paste was that its adherence properties were not great and we had to use gobs to make anything stick. I remember some of my papers had lumps under each corner. The paste would dry out quickly and contained dried out particles all through it which made it even more difficult to hold a paper chain together. Somehow, the paste eaters survived.

Arithmetic, as it was called in my youth, and math, as it's referred to now, never came easily to me, no matter what it was called. Or, at least, I thought a-r-i-t-h-m-e-t-i-c was shady. By the way, I learned to spell arithmetic, as many students did in 1950, by the idiom, "a rat in Tommy's house might eat Tommy's ice cream."

One morning, our teacher introduced the class to the process of "addition." After writing several practice examples on the board she asked for volunteers to walk to the slate chalkboard and add the correct answer. Okay, I understood that. Only I hoped she would not ask me to go up to the board. I didn't raise my hand. I didn't want to be tested on the fact unexpectedly.

As we were completing our addition assignments on our five-by-seven manila arithmetic papers, other students at my table seemed to figure out the answers more quickly than I. Usually I was confident that my answers were correct, but I always suspected that my classmates were applying some sort of secret method that I hadn't grasped yet in order to compute faster than I.

Pressure.

I lowered my head while peeking around to see if my classmates were done. I felt pressured to complete my math. I wasn't working fast enough.

What were my classmates doing that I wasn't?

Now remember, I wasn't about to raise my hand and tell the teacher that I didn't get it. I loved my teacher, but I lacked the self-confidence to admit in front of all my friends that I didn't comprehend something that they obviously did. I was just not brave enough yet.

So, in order to complete my addition work in a more timely fashion, I devised my own secret system of computation.

I used a series of "red dots" as visual cues to count in my head.

Little did I know that I created my own calculator complete with bright red dots. How ingenious was that?

Keep in mind, this was in the 1950s. Classrooms did not have an over abundance of teaching materials. We did not have concrete objects to help with "hands on learning" as many schools enjoy today; much of the learning was in the abstract form.

Luckily, I had one advantage. I unknowingly applied a skill I had used often at my house. You see my three sisters and I played a lot of card and board games while we were growing up on the farm.

I was very familiar with the characteristic placement of diamonds, hearts, spades, and clubs on decks of playing cards. So using the image of red dots, I created my own visual calculator in my head with rows of twos or threes. For "5 + 3 =" I would picture a number five card with two red dots on top, one dot in the middle, and two at the bottom. I could calculate quickly because I didn't have to count all five, I counted three more starting from the visualization of five in my head.

I used this secret calculating method all through elementary school. The sad part is I always felt as if I was doing something wrong, that perhaps I was cheating. Little did I know that I was employing my self-designed system of counting. Clearly, my guarded method was unique and successful.

I continued to feel guilty about having to resort to this gimmick and never revealed my dependence upon this resourceful instrument until much later in life.

Painfully, however, I thought I was unintelligent. For years I thought I was "slow" when it came to math. I constantly doubted my own abilities. Many kids doubt their own abilities.

Then, one day, all was right in Norma's math world. I was normal.

There it was in black and white, written on the pages of an instructional journal on *How to Teach Math in the Elementary Classroom*.

"Students will develop mental images which they need to use at the abstract level of number concepts."

Yes, Norma, had some normalcy. Hurrah. All those years, I was not crazy. Maybe I even used creative thinking with those red dots for my personal counting system.

It wasn't until I became an adult and began taking courses in methods of teaching elementary math, that I learned the importance of children using math manipulatives. Applying this knowledge of the importance of students touching actual materials, I covered my classroom math shelves with beans, bread tags, rocks, cubes, shells, marbles, and buttons.

One June, in preparation for our annual school field day, we three kindergarten teachers excitedly planned several games and relay events to play outside. One game that we chose was Giant Steps, a game we'd grown up playing. To our great surprise, the children stood quietly before us showing no reaction to our announcement.

"What's Giant Steps?" a student asked.

The three of us looked at each other with dismay. All of us were hit with the reality that we had indeed grown older and times certainly had changed.

"We are getting old. What's happened to the world when kids don't play Giant Steps anymore?" We sang out in disbelief.

"Has anyone here ever played Giant Steps before?"

"No."

"Well, you are going to learn a fun new game today."

Then, we got another surprise.

"You may take six baby steps."

"Mother may I?"

"Yes, you may."

However many of the children did not take six steps, as they counted aloud one, two, and three, four, five, six. Instead, they took too few, or too many.

Some of the students lacked the one-to-one correspondence skill necessary to play the game well. Now, one-to-one correspondence is basic to counting and we don't even think about it. We certainly don't sit down with our children and say, "Today, mommy is going to teach you about one-to-one correspondence."

This very important skill happens naturally through play especially through playing card or board games. When we count out cards for a game of Go Fish, we say one, two, three, and as we say each number, we lay down a card. Each number corresponds to one card. Older siblings often teach younger brothers and sisters by announcing, usually aloud, "Hey, you're not counting that right. Hey, mom, dad. Look how he is counting. That's not right. Here let me show you the right way."

Children who have not had many opportunities to play these games miss out on developing this very important foundation of math.

Other games to reinforce early math skills and get children outdoors are Red Light, Hopscotch, and Giant Steps, even making mud pies. Yes, mud pies. There's nothing more satisfying than patting moistened dirt into an old pie plate and setting it to dry in the sun.

Then, while it's baking in the sun, you go out into the field to pick daisies to embellish the top of your pie. Talk about one-to-one correspondence. One-by-one I would pluck each white petal and place it in the center of the pie, carefully counting each one.

Then, as I picked off the remaining stubs of the bright yellow center, I placed them in the position of honor in the center of the pie.

Now I know what you're thinking: not all children have access to a field as I did. But there are other household items children could use. Think about it.

Learning often means getting down on the ground and mucky. So let the preschoolers make mud pies and dandelion crowns. Let them collect rocks to sort, count, and line up by size. Let them pour water from one container to another in the tub. Let the older children use measuring cups in the tub, (not glass cups, please). Once, I let students practice pouring water into measuring cups in our classroom sink and suggested in a newsletter that parents allow their child to do this at home. One parent came into the classroom the next day and said in a joking but friendly manner, "You're the one responsible for my child getting my bathroom floor all wet. Thanks a lot."

We must remember that all children do not learn in the same way or at the same time. As parents, it's particularly important to understand that siblings might be raised in the same household and environment, but each has his/her own learning style. As educators, we must be varied enough in our delivery of information to allow and meet these individual needs in the classroom. It is not an easy task.

When a child has not experienced the real value of 1/2, 1/3, or 1/4, through hands-on experiences, the symbols on paper just don't make as much sense.

There's no greater joy for a retired teacher than unexpectedly meeting a former student in the grocery store or on the street. There's the usual sudden stop to gaze into each other's face. Then, the look of realization that we had spent a whole year together in the past is followed by hugs and the exchange of news of what has happened in each other's life.

One day, a former student who was entering her freshman year of high school returned to visit the classroom. After greeting me with a big hug, she said, "I'll never forget how you taught us our fractions by opening up Mrs. Salway's Pizzeria and pretending to eat pieces of pizza made of felt. Then, we ate real pizza. Every time we learned fractions in other grades, I remembered those felt pizza pieces."

I once had a former student approach me and admit apologetically, "I hope you won't take this the wrong way but I have to tell you something. When I had you for a teacher in kindergarten I thought you were old. Now I look at you and you seem so young that I can't believe I ever thought you were old because obviously you were not."

We never get tired of hearing those stories.

Children who are excited about learning and are able to share and transfer that learning back into the home environment help bridge an educational gap that often exists in too many communities. The close connections created between home and school must be fused in order to help our students expand their love of lifelong learning while forging ties to strengthen our educational system.

There can be no secrets about learning. We need to share any technique that works. Parents and teachers should work corroboratively for that purpose. A few years ago, I renamed Show & Tell to Share Time Math, in an attempt to help children observe and discover math in everyday life. Each child shared an item brought from home and told about its shape, or size, or pattern, or counted marbles in groups of tens. We even counted using red hearts on playing cards.

Run back to give one last hug.

Chapter Six
Case of the Uglies

"RRRRRR"

"RRRRRR"

The fog was still lifting as I stood outside during early morning recess duty. Upon hearing the lion-like roar, I looked up to see Mel racing down the hill behind the school. His arms were outstretched as if in flight, his fingers tense and bent upward in a claw position.

The bell rang signaling the end of recess. Students ran to fall into line with their respective classes.

"Grrrr, grrrrr," the blond-haired six-year-old grumbled.

The sound was a familiar one, as were the accompanying gestures. Whenever Mel was unable to control his temper or was upset, he would react in this manner.

"What's wrong, Mel?" I asked.

"I've got the uglies," he answered.

"Do you want to tell me about them?"

"No, I've just got the uglies," he replied.

"Well, let's leave them outside this morning." I suggested. "We don't want any uglies to get inside the building, do we?"

A smile of approval appeared on his face. He seemed delighted with the idea of uglies suddenly having a new connotation. I imagined them myself as being crawling insects with large heads and numerous legs. Upon entering the classroom, he proudly announced to his teacher that he had left the uglies outside. I can only imagine how he envisioned the invisible critters.

On subsequent occasions the uglies were thrown away deep down inside the wastebasket, hidden, and once stuffed into his pocket. I'm not sure where the catchy expression originated but the amazing fact was that although Mel was unable to control his anger, he could identify and redirect it.

During the remainder of the school year Mel made tremendous progress in learning to deal with the social and academic issues of the classroom environment and controlling his own behavior. Primarily this was due to the patience and dedication shown by his kindergarten teacher.

Once, this veteran teacher asked me to keep an eye on him while he was in "time out" for disrupting the class. He was not allowed to look at books during that time, but instructed to sit quietly for five minutes.

"Would you read a story to me?"

"I'm sorry I'm not able to read to you." I responded.

"That's okay, I can't read either," he said sadly.

At that, I had a difficult time holding my composure.

I held a book in front of my face to hide my smile. It's a seldom known fact that teachers often place books in front of their faces or make a quick turn-about to avoid being caught laughing at a situation when they should remain serious. Please keep this a secret and don't let on to your children that teachers do this for you might diminish a teacher's ability to be effective in classroom control.

Patience sometimes has a way of dwindling by the end of May, especially if the weather is hot, making both students and teachers more anxious for school to be over. It was on one of these hot, muggy days that the normally calm kindergarten teacher's patience began to wear thin. Mel became very disruptive in the classroom. Her frustration caused her to raise her voice, a rare occurrence. The two, teacher and child, were both upset with each other.

Quietly, she asked me to cover her room while she took Mel aside.

"I'm sorry, Mel," she whispered.

"Oh, that's okay," he replied softly, his eyes gazing up at her in wonder and love.

He reached for her hand. Together, they went outside where hand-in-hand they walked around the playground, a tender moment of forgiveness between teacher and child.

Parenting and teaching can be stressful jobs. Kids can be very forgiving when they know you care.

"I want to go home. I want my mama."

As the upset little boy spoke these words, he flung his chair across the room while tears of frustration streamed down his red cheeks.

These were angry words spouting forth from a very young pre-kindergarten student many years ago. His birthday was in October and he had just missed the October fifteenth deadline on which students must turn five years old to be eligible to enter school. So, chronologically, he was still four years old. As I cleared the room of other students, he fell limply in a chair and sobbed.

"You won't like me anymore, now," he whispered between sobs.

"Of course, I'll still like you. I don't like what you did, but I'll always like you." I said softly.

Looking up at me with big brown tear-stained eyes, he said, "You will?"

"Well, of course, I will," I reassured him.

I learned a huge lesson about how some children are unable to separate our disapproval with an action from our feelings about them. This particular child needed this reminder again and again.

With the cooperation of grateful parents, we were able to assist this precious child with support in dealing with his frustrations.

Chapter Seven
The World According to a Child

The teacher teaches. The child learns.

That's the way it's supposed to work.

The child teaches. The teacher learns.

That works, too.

As teachers, we strive to meet the individual needs of a child academically, emotionally and socially. Whether a primary, elementary, middle or high school teacher or parent, we all face the challenges of dealing with those needs every day.

Children often freely share experiences and true observations of life. If some parents knew about the stories and events their children shared, they would leave town, immediately.

"I saw them on the couch, once." Oops.

"I smelled pot out there."

"My uncle shot a deer last night."

We must open our ears, listen, and value the words of a

child. Sometimes, we are given more information than we care to hear, but we had better listen.

We must use those bits of wisdom to understand a child's world and way of thinking.

Children notice many things we don't. Children are constantly observing our actions, facial expressions, non verbal communication, our clothes, our jewelry, our shoes, our smells, our glasses, our teeth, our skin, zits, and wrinkles. They don't miss a great deal. Of course, in their constant observation of us, they could be forgetting to notice certain letters, words, math symbols. You get the message.

One morning, while I was greeting students, a bright bubbly little lass, looked down at my shoes exclaiming, "Mrs. S, why do you wear the same pair of shoes every day?"

Whew. I wasn't expecting that one.

As I gazed down at my brown scuffed toed Mary Janes with the thick rubber soles, I replied, "Well, I guess I do wear the same shoes every day because they are so comfortable."

Of course, in my head I'm thinking, "I'm not going to wear spikes. I had given up high heels years ago. But, also I can wear tights with these when the weather gets colder and I'm out on playground duty. Hmmm, I could use a new pair of shoes."

My thoughts were interrupted with her smug but innocent pronouncement, "My mother has a hundred pairs of shoes, and she wears a different pair every day to match her outfit."

Another lesson learned. Kids are checking out my shoes. Maybe I should put math facts or sight words on my shoes? Actually, I did this once, not to my shoes, but taped to a child's shoes. That poor child has never forgotten this shoe embellishment incident or the word either. I called the parents that afternoon to explain my zany action and my use of masking tape as an academic reinforcement tool.

Caution. If you are going to teach something in a zany way explain your educational reasons first or follow up with a phone call or note. It will save you from being at the receiving end of parent comparison talks. Of course, parents talk about teachers. Do you think teachers talk about parents?

Parents, please, refrain from discussing your personal thoughts about certain teacher oddities in the presence of your child.

Teachers, please refrain from discussing your personal thought about others in the presence of your students.

Number one professional rule of the teaching world: maintain confidentiality.

Shoes are not all students notice. They notice every part of your body. Many years ago, a wise veteran teacher told me that I should never wear big flashy pieces of jewelry because it might be distracting to certain students. The child might be so distracted by the shiny sparkling object around my neck that he or she could not focus on the lesson. For a long time, I tried to avoid wearing any bauble that might fall into that category. I gave up as students, parents, and other teachers started wearing the hip, large necklaces. However, it did make me stop and think.

As the round-faced little boy exited the common room, a small room extension beyond my classroom where parent volunteers worked with individual students, he lowered his head, stared at the floor, and shuffled his feet slowly. His body language told it all. He was not happy.

"What is wrong? Why the long face?"

With a pout, he expounded, "I don't know why I have to keep practicing these dumb old words. I read them at home and now I have to practice them some more."

Placing his hands upon his hips, he continued, "I'm just a kid you know."

I'm just a kid, you know.

These were powerful words spoken by this bright, articulate six-year-old.

I have never forgotten them. The child teaches. The teacher learns.

Yes, he is just a child. Yes, we do require him to complete homework and practice words. That is important.

But, his enlightening words gave me an instant view into the world of a child. He saw it differently. Did it mean I changed my mind and said, "Oh now, you don't have to practice those sight words."

Oh, no. I brought him over to me, put my arm around him and asked, "But you want to learn to read, right?"

"Yes."

"And you've already learned to read lots of words, right?"

"Yes."

"And how did you learn to do that?"

"By reading and practicing my words," he responded with a little grin. I sensed he knew where I was going with that line of questioning.

I'm just a kid, you know.

Years ago, while a new addition was being constructed at our small town elementary school, the whole school population was moved into eleven portable classrooms temporarily erected in the parking lot of the local high school during the summer months. At that time, kindergarten was half a day with morning and afternoon sessions. The classroom space was cramped but we made do with what we had.

One winter day, however, due to an impending storm, students from both sessions arrived in the morning, and all would be dismissed at noon.

There were close to thirty students present that morning all assembled in one space hardly big enough for half that number. Then add twenty-nine overstuffed backpacks, twenty-nine pairs of wet boots, twenty-nine heavy puffy parkas, twenty-nine pairs of ski pants all the same color and size, twenty-nine colorful hats, twenty-nine pairs of gloves and mittens, twenty-nine character lunchboxes, and twenty-nine home-school folders.

Added to the mix was the fact that it was the day before Christmas vacation began.

Now ideally all this gear would be hung neatly on several rows of hooks.

Note the word ideally. There were barely enough hooks to store gear for fifteen students let alone twice that many. The picture more resembled a thrift store just after a large amount of donated clothing had been delivered.

Kids were falling over themselves and all their gear. But I managed to keep the squirmy, over-excited students under control. At least I thought I did. As we were packing up preparing to go home the phone kept ringing with calls from the office. Calls needed to be made to make sure every child was on the right bus in case no one was at home. One child was crying because she couldn't find her mitten. A boy was arguing with another because he leaned against him. In the meantime, I was trying to stay patient and focused.

I could feel my face begin to grow warm as I multitasked talking sanely on the phone while gesturing with hand movements to squabbling students. I felt like a maestro conducting sections of an orchestra while trying to keep the symphony flowing. There were muffled trumpeting grumbles over disagreements and woodwind fluttering whines from the inability to find lost items.

At this point a little boy with a striped shirt and blond hair tapped my arm several times to garner my attention. With eyes wide open and a concerned look on his face he whispered loudly, "It's very hard to be a teacher with all these extra kids in the room, isn't it Mrs. S?"

"Yes, it is. You noticed."

"Yes, I did."

I swallowed. These were powerful words with a powerful message. Did this teacher learn a valuable lesson? Yes, indeed. A lesson I have never forgotten. I carry my heart on my sleeve, so I've been informed. I don't hide my feelings well. However the classroom was soon calm and composed.

This experience taught me to be more aware of my nonverbal mannerisms. Little pairs of eyes are constantly watching, observing, and not shy about commenting.

Spring had finally arrived. I could tell, because the mud on the playground was being tracked in all over the floor. That mud always emitted a peculiar odor that filled the classroom, a combination of pungent odors that made you wonder what was lurking in puddles. Kids were wearing boots to protect their feet from mud, not snow. As we were preparing to go outside for recess, a little girl marched up to me, wrapped her arms around my neck and looked me straight in the eyes.

"I stuck up for you last night, Mrs. S. My sister said something about you that wasn't nice, but I told her she was wrong. My sister said that you were old because your hands are all crinkly and blue. But, I told her you were not old. I told her that you were just born that way."

That piece of wisdom stuck. I was defended in such a sweet manner that I'll love that child until the day I die. Immediately I peered down at my once smooth hands. My polished nails could not distract from the little lines and bluish veins. However, I'll never look at those veins popping out from the top of my thin aging hands quite the same ever again. The truth spoken by little ones sometimes hits hard in the vain department. This pun was not intentional.

As the weather improved that spring, we welcomed a chance to wear lighter clothing as days brought higher temperatures. With those increased temperatures, however, came the exposure of more skin to keen eyes than during the long Maine winters.

Pin-wheeling first graders were lining up waiting for me to apply sun screen before we ventured outside for our annual school field day events during the last week of school. It was very hot. I had dressed for the occasion with a white short sleeved shirt and khaki shorts.

Spring temperatures in Maine don't allow for much sun. To say that my legs and arms were somewhat pale was putting it mildly. As I slathered the lotion on a child, I heard a loud scream.

"Mrs. S. there's something on the back of your leg. Oh, look. It's awful."

I turned my head around and glanced down at the back of my left leg. I didn't see anything.

"Where is it? I don't see anything." *After all, it wasn't April Fool's Day.*

"Look. There. Behind your knee. It looks like a spider."

Oh, it was a spider all right. It was a spider vein. I have an obvious unattractive one on the back of my left knee. From the expressions on eighteen little faces, I sensed my little spider was now the center of attraction as curious girls and boys shifted closer to get a look.

"Oh, that. It's just a sign of getting older," I sighed. "It's nothing to worry about."

The little girl patted my shoulder, and said with a sympathetic tone, "I feel bad for you, Mrs. S."

"Oh, don't feel bad. It's part of aging. Let's go outside and enjoy the relay races, now," I suggested as I gave her a quick squeeze. I didn't want her to feel bad about her public announcement of the unsightly discovery.

Meanwhile, I pondered the need to purchase Capri pants to cover my knees.

In a kid's world they also think that teachers know the answer to every question.

"Do snakes have noses? What is the longest word in the whole world? Can you put your tongue on your nose?"

"Can you wriggle your nose?"

I always surprised my students when I displayed my ability to wriggle my nose like a rabbit. Of course there was always the fear of the principal suddenly appearing in the doorway.

One fall day, as I stood on the playground watching my students, a little boy with a striped shirt came running up to me flapping his outstretched arms wildly up and down. He stood there flapping and flapping. As he flapped, he twirled around in circles. He landed again in front of me very out of breath.

"Mrs. S., Mrs. S. May I ask you something?" Oh. Oh. Here it comes. I knew from experience when this well informed child asked me a question, it was usually a zinger.

All the while he was asking his question, he continued to sweep his arms up and down.

"Mrs. S. (huff, puff) how fast does a bird (huff, puff) flap its wings?"

"Well," I responded. "I'm not sure but that's a great question."

"Well, I need to know because I want to fly, too." he responded.

"You do? I always wanted to fly when I was your age." I confessed. Actually, I often would dream of flying over treetops wearing a power pack strapped to my back. I didn't admit that bit of information about myself as I didn't want to be responsible for any future misfortunes this revelation might cause.

You never know what a child is thinking. You also never know what lasting memories a student carries with them forever after spending a year together in the same classroom.

I have vivid memories about one of my elementary teachers. My eighth grade teacher always smelled of ginger snaps. We all knew that she kept a box of these cookies on a shelf behind her desk. As a result, she would scatter the aroma of ginger snaps wherever she walked.

To this day, whenever I smell ginger snaps, I think of this tall, slim lady who wore bright red nail polish on her long fingernails and wore her hair up in a bun. She also had a habit of reaching down inside her dress to haul up her slip strap while standing before the entire class teaching English.

Why do I still remember this oddity after more than fifty years? Somehow I think it was a reaction to her long red nails and the possibility that she might scratch herself. However it was not only the pulling on her strap I remember. She somehow managed to instill in her students a love of English and the language arts, along with diagramming sentences and a fondness for ginger snaps. Unfortunately one day someone stole her box of ginger snaps and the unsolved incident left the cookie memory stale.

I mention these stories to remind those who rarely venture into an elementary classroom that there is more churning around in the world of our students than academic facts. Perhaps if we devote as much time to the emotional distress of some of our students and families in our violent society, and less on testing, we can reach kids before it's too late.

Today is Picture Day!
NKS

Chapter Eight
Surprises

Unexpected events happen in the classroom more often than at home, simply because there are more little people involved. New haircuts cause shame or sheer joy. Shoes are too tight; shoes are too loose; buckles and strings break. Favorite beads break all over the floor. Perfume is shared. Perfume is spilled. "That stinky smell is giving me a headache."

Note to self: tell students not to bring cologne to school.

Boots are misplaced, mistaken, lost. Mittens are lost. Hats are lost. Pencils are lost. Belts break. Pants are too loose. Where is some twine? Tights rip. Pets die. Family members die. New brothers and sisters are born. New pets join families.

"Why are you so sad this morning?"

"My mom and dad are getting a divorce."

"You need a hug."

"Can I bring my new pig in for Show and Tell?"

I'd better take attendance. The office will be calling.

"Oh, no."

Milk is spilled. Paint is tipped over. Toilets overflow. Hair gets tangled. Hair is covering eyes. Scissors cut items other than paper.

"Why did you cut your bangs?"

"They were in my eyes."

Band aides for scraped knees. Band aides for cuts. Band aides to cover emotional bruises.

Could you walk to the office please and ask for more band aides? Don't forget to wear our hallway pass.

"I hate what she packed for my lunch. My mom knows I don't like bologna, but she packs it anyway. I'm hungry."

"Mom didn't pack my hat."

"Dad packed my things today. I don't have my note. I don't have my homework."

Pencil lead breaks. Crayons break.

Who sharpened their crayon in the pencil sharpener?

Glue won't come out. Glue is spilled.

"Our dog got sprayed by a skunk last night."

"What's that smell in here? I think I'm going to puke."

"Raise your hand if you want the first lunch choice. Raise your hand for the second lunch choice. Raise your hand if you're having cold lunch."

"Why didn't you raise your hand?"

"I don't know."

Parents oversleep. Busses break down. Students arrive late.

"What do want for lunch?"

The office calls.

"Where is your daily attendance folder and hot lunch count, Mrs. S?"

Not to diminish the relevance of any of these matters, I must point out that the most common electrifying happening in any primary classroom is caused by a small pointy white miracle of life. We exclaim when our baby cuts their first one. We exclaim when the first one falls out. In the meantime, the drama unfolds each time a tooth leaves the mouth of a child in one form or another. Why is it that teeth wait until the child arrives at school to decide to make their exit?

You know that some parents refer to their adorable child as the "drama queen."

You know when that child's tooth is wiggly and unforgiving there will be drama in the classroom. Often this drama continues for several days until the final departure.

It helps to keep some perspective in the matter and remember what it was like when we were in that stage of development.

So I would usually share with my students my own personal agonizing but highly spirited tales of losing my teeth. (Children of all ages beg to hear stories about our growing up escapades.)

There it was sticking out of the front of my mouth. This small white front tooth hanging by a thread protruding out interfering with everything that entered my mouth. I wouldn't attempt to eat an apple, because I didn't want my tooth to break off. Even when I tried to talk, my upper lip pressed against the side of the little white object forcing me to wince in pain. As my eyes watered from the crunchy impact, I covered my mouth quickly with my hand to ease the ache. Oh, how I wished this tooth would just fall out!!

We all remember those moments when we were six, going on seven, when this miracle of dental development caused us so much misery. Some things we just don't forget. For at least a week or more, I would chew on one side of my mouth very slowly to avoid biting down on the precious baby partner I'd brushed and cared for since infancy. I wanted this tooth to stay with me forever. But, now I wanted it out of my mouth this minute!

As a mother and a teacher, I could sympathize with my children and students as they passed through this wondrous but fretful stage of life. With each loss of a white baby pearl, we came closer and closer to growing up. With each loss unfortunately, came stories of precious teeth being accidently swallowed or lost in a mound of spaghetti or at the edge of the playground in the gravel.

In any primary grade classroom, the loss of a tooth was a common occurrence. However, that event never lost its importance or the drama.

The cries of a sobbing child broke the silence in the empty schoolroom while students enjoyed the morning recess in the warm spring air. Holding her blood covered hand over her mouth, the little girl rushed to the bathroom sink at the end of the long hallway with brightly painted yellow bead board lining the walls.

"I lost my tooth!" Sob, sob. "I lost my tooth on the ground and I'll never find it and I can't put it under my pillow and the tooth fairy won't come." Sob. Sob.

In a kind nurturing manner, her teacher came to the rescue with words to console and reassurance that she could write a note to the tooth fairy telling her what had happened to her tooth. This conversation, however, was not lost on our friendly custodian with a soft spot for kids.

"I will go outside and look for it," he gently announced to the distressed lass. "I have very sharp eyes!"

A while later, this tall gentleman with a broad smile and gray hair, entered the classroom where the little girl sat and held up his hand. Held carefully between his thumb and index finger was a tiny, shiny, pointed white object.

"My tooth! My tooth! You found my tooth! Oh, thank you, thank you!" she joyfully called out as she wrapped her arms around his legs in a big hug.

Her teacher placed the tooth inside a small white envelope, sealed it tightly, and then wrote the child's name on the front.

"How did you ever locate that tooth in all the gravel?" I asked our custodian later that day as he was sweeping the walkway. "You must really have sharp eyes to spot that tooth."

"Isn't it amazing how all those tiny white pointy pebbles resemble little white pointy teeth?" he chuckled with a twinkle in his eyes and giving me a wink.

One morning, a normally social and talkative little fellow entered our grade one classroom. He hurried quietly to his cubby and hung up all his winter gear and backpack. Without saying a word, he walked over to my desk and handed me his home-school folder.

"Good morning, Gary. How are you today?"

Without a reply, he quickly turned and walked away avoiding any chance to be questioned further. As other students entered and became socially engaged in conversation and play, I noticed that Gary chose to sit at his desk building alone with math unifix cubes.

"Mrs. S. there's something wrong with Gary. He will not talk to anyone. He just nods his head up and down to say he's okay, but he won't talk to me."

This was rather unusual for Gary as he was known for chatting incessantly.

I reached for Gary's home-school folder. Inside, there was a note from his mom that read:

"Gary has a very loose tooth. He refused to eat his breakfast this morning. I hope he or his tooth don't cause any problems at school today. The tooth should fall out soon. I hope he will eat something during snack time."

Not only did he refuse to eat a snack, he refused to open his mouth at all the entire day. He would not talk to anyone. He would not eat this lunch. He would not read aloud during reading group. In fact, much of the time, he held his hand over his mouth. We all tried pleading and coaxing him to open his mouth. We knew he had a loose tooth. Several of his friends offered their advice and stories about their personal loose tooth episodes. But he remained stoic and silent. He did sip some milk from a straw out of one corner of his mouth at lunch time.

After the students were dismissed and busses departed, I made a phone call to mom explaining Gary's silent mode and lack of any solid nutrition. She assured me that she too would continue to have a chat with her starving son. We both wished for that tooth to come out. However, we both agreed that it was most peaceful at home and in the classroom.

The next morning, Gary entered the classroom with a big grin. However, it was not a holey grin. The loose tooth was sticking out—just barely attached. But Gary was talking! Oh, was he ever. He began to tell all his friends about his terribly loose tooth.

In the meantime, I reached into his folder to retrieve a note from mom. It read:

"The mystery has been solved. It seems that Gary had been told the previous morning, "You will probably LOSE that tooth today because it is ready to POP out!"

He had taken the cautionary warning literally. He told his parents that he was afraid that if he opened his mouth, his tooth would FALL OUT and be LOST! He was not familiar with the use of the words, "losing a tooth." He thought the tooth would pop out of his mouth and be LOST forever. How would he have the tooth to place under his pillow if it was lost?

That night, the tooth finally came out and the Tooth Fairy made her rounds according to the written account in a new note from mom the following morning.

One of my warmest surprise recollections of my teaching days happened on school photo day. Boys and girls arrived smelling of soap and shampoo and dressed in their picture day finery or sometimes regular clothing. A sweet-natured round-faced little boy stepped through our classroom door wearing a grin on his shiny face and two neckties around his neck. Surprise.

"Just look at you. You look terrific all dressed up with your two ties!" I said.

"I couldn't decide which one to wear. So, I wore both of them!" he replied.

With suggestions from his friends, he did decide on one tie before our class was called to the gym. However, the innocent and spontaneous naturalness of that image was planted in my heart and brings forth joy these many years later.

These small special surprise moments linger.

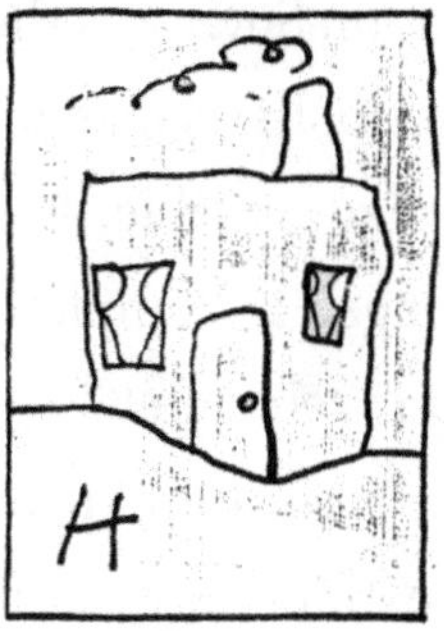

Chapter Nine
Look Before You Sit

Any parent knows that if you have toddlers learning the art of using the toilet, the seat is not always clean. You check before you sit. Of course those fortunate to have a master bath and separate child bathrooms don't have to worry as much. Teaching the basics in reading, writing, and arithmetic is very important in a classroom. However, lessons in hygiene and toilet etiquette often get top billing. Any elementary school teacher knows that bathroom issues can pop up at any moment. Keep in mind that some schools have separate girls and boys bathrooms located down the hall from the classroom. Others have one generic facility inside the classrooms. Both offer unique opportunities for student exploration and activity other than that which a privy is intended.

For some reason children think once they close the door to their inner sanctum, their voices are inaudible to the rest of the world, their peers, or to the teacher who is quietly working in the classroom. Such was the case one morning during reading group. I was listening to a group of first grade students at the reading table. The remaining students were at their seats engaged in completing daily assignments. The classroom was relatively quiet.

Suddenly from the bathroom I heard the rousing rendition of an opera. The exuberant voice rose to a crescendo with high fidelity notes echoing throughout the classroom. I looked toward the closed door as the music continued to fill the classroom which had become unusually quiet. As my eyes scanned the quizzical faces, I discovered that all eyes were focused on ME. Without saying a word, I knew what they were thinking. The tra-la-las grew louder and more vibrato.

What was she going to do?

What I did was nothing but smile.

All eighteen students smiled back without saying a word. Joyous silence filled the room for we all knew something remarkable had just occurred.

This student who had just blessed us with a solo performance rarely spoke in class. The students understood that what they heard was a gift. We were hearing that child's voice as never before with all the gusto and melody flowing so easily.

Then all was quiet in the bathroom. We heard the flush. The door opened. The child entered the classroom, looked over at me, smiled and returned to work.

I'm sure later on the playground I overheard someone

say to that child, "We could hear you singing in the bathroom, you know."

A broad smile; that was the child's only response.

Now, I've heard many songs emitted from the bathroom from "I Get Around" by the Beach Boys, the "Alphabet Song," "Happy Birthday," "The Wheels on the Bus" and more. However, the musical performances usually don't continue once the secret is revealed and everyone knows that what is sung in the bathroom doesn't stay in there. Sound travels. Who knew?

Behind the door of the girls' bathroom located near my desk, I once overheard bits and pieces of a conversation. The audible chatter continued for quite some time. As the little girl emerged from completing her duties, I asked if she had been talking with someone in the adjoining bathroom.

"No. I was talking to myself. I always talk to myself. It helps me feel not lonely."

This was memorable advice freely expressed from the heart of a six-year-old and advice I've never forgotten. Try talking to yourself, or to God, or to the cat. It will help you feel not lonely.

One day I was sent home from school. Not when I was a child, but as an adult.

I was working at a small rural school as a teacher's aide prior to getting my teaching degree. The schoolhouse was an older building that had seen many renovations in its long history. There were three separate bathrooms with single seats therein. One was located in the kindergarten room and used by girls and boys. In the back of the building, at the end of the long hallway, there was a small boys' bathroom on the right (with an old wooden one-holer hidden behind a door) and a girls' bathroom on the left. In between the two was my little office area.

Every day after lunch I had playground duty. After finishing lunch, I proceeded to the rear of the building to use the girls' bathroom. Since I was running late, I quickly lowered myself onto the customary cold, hard seat.

Something did not feel right. In fact, something warm and squishy was oozing uncomfortably around the seat.

"Oh, no." I screamed. I had sat down in……. It was so bad that it squished down all over my clothes. How had I not noticed the odor when I ventured in?

My teaching colleagues heard my screams and came to see what had happened. They stood outside the bathroom door and uttered pleas of helplessness and dismay.

Needless to say I was sent home for the rest of the day to take a long, long shower and change my clothes.

I learned a lifelong lesson that day. Always look before you sit.

Parents and teachers listen carefully to what I'm going to tell you. You need to know where the shut off valve is located on a toilet. This should be part of both teacher and parent training. If there are kids around, you must know this plumbing skill. You will not learn about this skill in any teacher manual. Since most modern classrooms now have separate bathroom facilities, the chances of the toilet being plugged and overflowing increases with each additional student. Some years you will have one of those students who can't seem to stop wadding the paper into a snowball shape, no matter how much you lecture on the subject. When the toilet is plugged, there is no time to call the custodian. You need to be able to wade into the water and turn the knob behind the toilet. Unless of course, it has a key and the key is nowhere in sight.

It was always embarrassing to hear over the intercom, "Would a custodian please report to Mrs. S's classroom immediately." We all knew what that school-wide announcement meant. The crisis usually was caused by vomit or water.

The students squealed with delight to see a pig at school.

Chapter Ten
Excuses

There is no teaching or parenting manual that prepares you for the pleasure of being the beneficiary of excuses, in both verbal and written testimonies. However, justifications for one's actions comes in pleas, stalls, regrets, and all sorts of written forms for certifying absences, illnesses, or failure to complete assignments. Some of the best explanations are quickly manufactured improvisations for misconduct delivered by caught-in-the-act cherubs.

"I was at my cousin's house and we got home too late and then my little brother threw up all over it."

We've heard many creative excuses for not completing homework assignments, but often the reasons are simply "life takes over."

"He dedn do hez homwrk cuz he coudn finde it."

In this case an older brother tried to provide the excuse.

Often work would come back covered with coffee, juice, or chocolate stains, or taped with duct tape with a note saying, "Sorry, we didn't have regular tape."

I chuckled. At least the child finished the assignment.

However, once I found myself having to compose an excuse to a parent.

One evening after correcting writing prompts at the kitchen table, I carefully placed the stack of student work inside my big teacher tote bag. I placed the stuffed bag on top of the washing machine near my purse and lunch bag ready for the morning departure.

During the night my curious Maine coon cat, Gusty, obviously had climbed inside the bag. How did I know? There in the bag, the next morning, were shards of paper chewed from student writings.

"Gusty. Look what you did."

Of course this inquisitive feline came running when he heard his name and curled his tail under my chin demanding a scratch.

"What do I tell the parents? Do I tell them my cat ate their child's work?"

That's what I did. After all, it was the truth. After taping together the tattered pieces, I attached a note apologizing for the cat damaging the child's writing project he/she had so diligently created. The surprised child doubled over in laughter upon seeing the note.

One fall morning during a warm spell, a brown-eyed lad quietly entered the classroom. With his head lowered, he went over to his coat hook to hang up his jacket. It was obvious through his body language that he was not happy.

Still wearing his red knit cap, he walked over to me and placed his Home-School Folder in my hand.

"My mom put a note in my folder," he said in soft voice.

This was unusual behavior since this particular child usually was quite chatty early in the morning and eager to converse with his friends. I sensed that under that cap was a new haircut.

As I pulled out the note, the little boy studied my face to see how I would react to his mother's message.

"Dear Mrs. Salway,

Please excuse Dan if he insists on wearing his hat throughout the school day. He is very unhappy with his new, too short haircut and has not taken his hat off since leaving the barber.

He even slept with his hat on. I hope this does not cause any problems in the classroom. I'll be home if there is a problem."

"It's okay, Dan, when you're ready to take off your hat, you may."

Three days later he removed his hat.

"Yeah, Dan took off his hat," his friends cheered.

He smiled and strode off to play.

During my first year of teaching, I received this note:

"Dear Mrs. Salway,

Did you really tell Barry that it was okay to bring in his pig for Show and Tell?

He said you did. I will bring it in on Friday morning if that is okay."

I had heard lots of stories about this pig. The little boy had pleaded with me to allow him to bring his little pig to school. After questions about size and transportation issues, I said he could, if his mother agreed.

Friday morning arrived. Soon there was a commotion in the hallway.

"She's here. My mom is here with my little pig."

I opened the door.

There coming down the hall was this poor mother with this rather large pig.

"Did Barry tell you how big his pig is?" she groaned as she tugged at the snorting pig.

"Well, he told me he wasn't very big," I replied with an apologetic stammer. I also noticed a rather pig-like aroma filling the hallway. Nearby classroom doors began to open as teachers and students glared and chuckled at this unusual school visitor.

The pig entourage entered the room as the students squealed with delight to see a pig at school. The pig squealed with delight to see his young master at school. The mom sat down in utter amazement and teased me something in the tone of, "Are you crazy?"

To this day the mother and I exchange remembrances of the day the pig came to school. We always hug when we meet, forever bonded by a pig.

Parents do your homework when your child begs for a little pet. Actually, I'm not sure the pig was a pet. I think he might have ended up in the freezer.

However, times have changed and many schools no longer allow creatures in the classroom.

Teachers, take your students to farms, zoos, and wildlife parks or to the fair in the fall. Parents, let them scramble for their own little pig. Keep in mind how large they can become.

Once in a while circumstances arise that cause children to respond with the skill, wisdom, and articulation of an adult. These children are wise beyond their young years, and have the uncanny ability to think fast on their squirming feet. Often this swiftness of thought is to assist them in getting out of a perilous situation, often involving confrontation with a parent or a teacher. In other words, he/she has broken a rule and was trying to wiggle a way out of it-resulting in a creative, spontaneous excuse.

How we respond to growing-up imperfections and resulting excuses is the lesson here. Anticipate that busy parents, mischievous children, failed alarm clocks, curious pets, stalled ignitions, and our own fluffs and blunders will temporarily enlighten our lives.

In late May our school annually celebrates the fine arts by transforming the walls in our hallways into an impressive art gallery. Colorful, creative student illustrations line the concrete block walls. Each student has at least two samples of their endeavors. The art teacher, along with a group of parent volunteers, spends hours taping and hanging the display for parents, students, and the public to view.

Keep in mind that schools have hallways that students use to travel from their classrooms to music, art, computer, and physical education classrooms. Keep in mind that in order to arrive at these destinations, children are instructed to walk quietly so as not to disturb other classrooms in session. Remember also that long halls with long walls are most enticing to students. Children are very tactile and love the feel of painted concrete blocks and how their fingers feel traveling down into the grout lines, as if following paths and roads. Some of you have done that.

Knowing the temptation of students to travel these sensory paths, we constantly remind these curious creatures to "keep your hands off the wall."

Along with daily reminders are suggestions to respect all the work involved in the creation of these art masterpieces, and the caution of accidently ruining someone's prized painting by carelessly running a hand over the edges resulting in a rip. Oh, yes, spoken from experience.

On this warm late-May afternoon, I readied my eighteen students for a long walk from my first grade classroom to the music room located at the other end of the building. I began with giving the usual reminders about the walls being covered with students' work and the importance of keeping our hand off the walls. I usually led the way walking alongside the student designated "line leader." Occasionally, I would walk backwards to check on the end of the line where trouble often bubbled. We arrived at the door of the music room uneventfully and the students filed in and sat down.

Forty minutes later, after spending that time stuffing student mailboxes and Home-School Folders, I returned to escort the students back to our classroom and to prepare our belongings for departure. Before leaving the music room however, I gave one quiet reminder about keeping our hands off the walls and relating how well they had done on the walk down to music.

We walked briskly along with me in the lead and the students in a line behind.

I always felt like a mother duck with her charges waddling behind. Never knowing when one would fall out of line, I stopped occasionally and turned around to observe.

Just as I turned around, I caught the eye of a bright little boy as he quickly removed his hands from sweeping across the row of illustrations.

He knew he was in my sight as our eyes met.

Saying nothing, I walked slowly toward him and threw both my hands up into the air.

Translation: "What were you thinking? What were you doing?"

With his dark eyes dancing and sparkling, I could sense his little brain thinking overtime. He gazed up at me with those big eyes widening as I walked ever closer to his side. Then he spoke, stammering and stuttering his carefully chosen words.

"Ah, ah, well, I was, I was humming, Mrs. S, and the humming took my memory away." He tapped his forehead to emphasize his lack of concentration.

Profound. Most creative excuse I'd heard in all my years of teaching.

Chapter Eleven
Tools of the Trade

My mom lived through the Depression so the words "make do" were part of our vocabulary from the time we were old enough to drop clothespins into a milk carton, play marbles using the floor register as the marble pot, or paint on cardboard. We grew up in an atmosphere where we were encouraged to make something out of practically any leftover materials found around the farm. Unfortunately, or fortunately, this gift can lead to the making of a packrat, or collector. But, most importantly, the stimulation of more powerful forces is cultivated: imagination and invention. I also grew up with the mantra, "You had better save that for you might need it someday."

I recently went down in history by a moving company for shattering the record of the client having the most stuff to move. It was not exactly presented with bragging rights, either. I down-sized, too, before packing all those boxes. Past experience and love of everything old molded my life from such an early age, that the process was compounded by saving many tubs labeled vintage books, vintage aprons, vintage linens, vintage clothing, vintage toys.

For a child growing up in that environment, who chooses to be a teacher, it's leverage for augmenting materials in the classroom. It can also be helpful for parenting as long as you realize that creativity and messiness often embrace the productive child. I've learned, too, that in the process of creating, I am often inattentive to what is going on around me. You must know a child such as me. I have a friend who cautions that it's a good thing that her daughter and I don't live in the same household.

Mom also taught us that, "Necessity is the mother of invention." As a parent and teacher, we become most proficient at repurposing household materials to patch, clean, fasten, mend, rebuild, and reinvent. Stored in the bottom drawer of my teacher desk, along with my secret stash of little squares of chocolate (to reboot teacher energy) are rolls of duct tape, masking tape, a screw driver, small hammer, safety pins, needle and thread, and string. Tape can be most accommodating in an emergency.

One evening my kindergarten-teaching-colleague and I were preparing for our annual Kindergarten Parent's Night. As we were arranging the refreshment table, she suddenly revealed to me, "I hate to tell you but the hem of your skirt has come undone and it's hanging down."

With only a few minutes remaining before parents started arriving, we grabbed the masking tape we had used for hanging posters and quickly taped up the dragging hem. Of course worrying about the longevity of the tape's ability to stay stuck on material only added to my anxiety level while talking before the crowd of parents.

But the tape held up the hem until I got home.

Another time, a brown-haired little girl was skipping around the playground when her patent leather shoe went flying. She was wearing heavy leotards and the strap on the shoe just ripped apart. Her foot squished down into muddy ground while she fetched her shoe from under the wooden bench.

"Can you fix my shoe, pleeeeeease? My mother is not going to be happy. These are my new tights, too, and now they're all muddy."

Once inside I instructed the other students to finish their morning work while I attempted to tape the strap tight enough so the shoe would not come off again. Luckily the rip was in the center of the strap and held up fairly well.

Another time I was not as lucky as the rip on the strap was at the small buckle end, and we had to wrap the tape beneath the shoe. This temporary fix didn't last.

Usually once or twice a year there will be the lunch box dumping caused by a broken hinge. Duct tape to the rescue.

Straps on overalls break and fancy headbands. Now you would think a teacher's day is filled with academics. Hold on. These are lessons in how to cope with minor obstacles. Every child needs to learn how to problem solve. They need to learn to "make do."

One day the whole sole on the bottom of a pair of sneakers came off. Now that problem I could not fix with duct tape. Mom was called to bring in an extra pair of shoes.

Yarn is also a household and classroom staple you don't read about in a teaching manual.

My advice is to go to yard sales and buy balls of yarn to keep in your emergency bag, at home or at school. Yarn can be used for hundreds of purposes from creating a belt to hold up a pair of pants to stringing spelling-word necklaces. One year, a parent sent in several skeins of colored yarn. What a hit. One skein was left in the art/writing center for children to use for making books, ornaments, tags, signs, bracelets, or to just tie packages. It was great for hanging art from the ceiling or measuring pumpkins.

Ribbon is treasure to children and cats. It enhances our lives with its flexibility, variations, colors, and useful purpose, just as yarn does. Give a child a piece of ribbon and it can be transformed into fashionable items. Such was the case in my classroom.

In my younger days of teaching I would wear a narrow strand of grosgrain ribbon in my hair tied with a small bow at the top. Usually I chose a color to match whatever I was wearing. It was nothing flamboyant, just a thin band to keep hair out of my face.

One rainy morning when we were stuck inside for recess, a girl with long brown hair asked me for a piece of ribbon. Reaching into my "ribbon, yarn, and string" cubbie, I asked what color she wanted.

"I want the same color as yours," she replied. "I'd like red. Could you tie it around my head like you do?"

With a red ribbon tied around her hair, she proudly walked over to display her new fashion trend to her peers. Before the recess was over, eight little girls were wearing red ribbons in their hair, tied with a bow at the top, just like their teacher. Oh, the sweet bond of bows.

"That's not fair." I heard a little boy exclaim.

"Well, we can fix that. Would you like a ribbon in your hair?" I asked.

He quickly declined the offer.

Recycled paper scraps can be catalysts to spark invention. I've been known to raid the teacher's room for odd sizes of construction and copy paper, sometimes pulling them out of the garbage.

After cutting off any print, I'd turn what was leftover into pages for books, or practice paper for spelling words. The same can be done at home. Save suitable junk mail and have a child cut it into grocery or reminder lists. Staple or tie the pages together at the top and you have an instant memo pad. Students can make these for you when their work is done. They make great gifts, too.

Kids of all ages love junk. In the eyes of a visionary child, a recycled paper towel tube can be transformed into unlimited gadgets or toys. We need to provide tools to generate imagination in our children. I repeat, those tools do not have to be expensive. They are as close as the outdoors or the recycle bin. Junk mail provides an abundance of possibilities.

The recent death of Steve Jobs reminded all of us of the importance of vision and imagination. One of my favorite quotes is from Albert Einstein. He once said, "Imagination is more important than knowledge."

As parents and teachers we must strive to ignite the spark of self-learning by providing tools and opportunities to create and put into practice knowledge gained from the classroom experiences. I repeat again, these creative tools do not have to cost money. One of my favorite lessons in creativity was provided by my mom back in the 1950s. She showed my sisters and me how to fold a sheet of newspaper into a sailor hat. I've been repurposing junk ever since.

Nature, with all its marvels, often provides an abundance of teaching materials.

It was Memorial weekend and the anticipation of the end-of–the school year had already caused some children to "pack it up." The yearning for lazy summer days had settled into the behaviors and attitudes of many students long before the last day of school. Teachers were challenged on a daily basis to keep behaviors in check and delivery of academics more stimulating than ever. It was the time of year when students were constantly distracted by new sunburns and insect bites and the fear of ticks. Tick checks were now conducted routinely upon reentering the classroom after outside recess.

There's nothing more alarming for a child than finding a tick crawling up their leg.

"Get it off me. Get it off me, quick, quick!"

You can imagine the scene when this occurs during a math lesson.

With this in mind, it was the perfect time to provide one of nature's marvelous specimens for students to observe while reinforcing and enriching our science curriculum. There's nothing more symbolic of developing children than the life cycle of a frog and the miracles of metamorphosis. It was time to delve into the waters of Songo Pond, the small lake I viewed each morning out my kitchen window, for the search for the perfect creature, a two year old, chubby, wiggly tadpole, just beginning to form legs.

Early one morning that holiday weekend, I walked down to the dock as the sun shone brightly onto the shallow waters near our small beach. Tadpoles swam lazily in the warm waters, occasionally one coming up for air. Slowly, I sprawled out on my belly on top of the dock and whispered to myself, "People riding by in their cars are going to think I'm crazy." Here I was with a kitchen strainer held up in my hand lying prone on the dock.

I watched and waited for the biggest, fattest, most developed pollywog to swim near. I was careful not to cast my shadow onto the calm waters and spook them. A large oversized pickle jar sat nearby filled with fresh pond water and microorganism nutrients. Then I saw him—the perfect pollywog for observation in my classroom. It already had back legs and developing forelimbs. Slowly, I lifted the strainer for a quick scoop into the water. Splash! I brought up the net, but there was no pollywog inside. I waited for the water to settle and once again become calm.

I was aware of passing motorists and bicyclists casting glances at this weird lady. What was she doing?

I wanted to shout, "Hey, I'm a teacher preparing a science lesson. I'm working!"

But I was too busy tracking the movements of the star of the lesson to worry what people thought.

Then, I saw it again. This time, I had to be faster with my swoop. I watched and waited for him to swim closer as I inched my way to the edge of the old dock. Then, the moment arrived. I reached out and quickly scooped the strainer into the water and brought it up quickly with the wiggly tadpole successfully inside. I carefully lowered him into the large container that would be the observation tank for students.

What excitement the next morning as the children discovered the visitor on our classroom science table.

We read stories about tadpoles. Students created drawings of the life cycle of a frog and labeled the parts and stages. They asked many questions and wrote their own stories and little books. At the end of the day, the tadpole returned to its home in the pond, but the enthusiasm continued as children told me stories of finding their own eggs and pollywogs at home.

A little girl with long curly hair gazed up at me and said, "Someday, I want to be a teacher so I can bring pollywogs into my classroom, too. "

Then, one year, this annual lesson came to an end.

There were no more pollywogs to be found in the lake. Why, I wondered?

However, the little girl with curly hair taught me to never underestimate the power of the lasting influences of connections with nature. The sparks of inspiration and learning can abound in the simplest of materials, such as a wiggly creature in a pickle jar.

Look up often for dinosaurs in the sky.

Chapter Twelve
Let Them Write

"My smile is full of holes."

These words were written in a journal by a seven year old. They brought a smile (with all my teeth) to my face as I read. As a first grade teacher I was used to seeing smiles full of holes as losing teeth was often a daily occurrence in our classroom. One of the joys of teaching for me was reading about the personal experiences of my students in their journals, as recorded in hand printed letters using inventive spelling. Our journals were not fancy but manila paper, lines on the bottom, with a space at the top for an illustration.

The journal entries provided me with a glimpse into a child's personal world. Sometimes I'd laugh out loud. Sometimes, I would cry. Sometimes, I'd sigh. Sometimes, I'd gather valuable clues about skill lessons I needed to teach. Often, I would write responses to concerns in the margins. Sometimes, I would be amazed at the clarity of voice in those words. Nothing revealed more about the deep feelings and passions within my young students. Keep in mind these early writing attempts at words and sentences were not spelled correctly. Often I had to hold additional discussions with children to uncover the mystery of some of the spellings. There has been a huge debate about encouraging the use of inventive spelling in very young students.

One morning during journal time a student asked how to spell the word "remont." Not understanding the word, I asked her if she would use it in a sentence, to which she replied, "Over the weekend, we went to visit our friends in 'remont,' not Maine, but another state."

Ever since I began teaching, I enjoyed teaching students to write, play with letters and sounds, knowing that when children write naturally, using invented spelling, they are able to make the transition into the world of reading much easier. That is not to say that children should not learn how to spell correctly. THEY SHOULD. But even children in kindergarten and first grade could communicate their thoughts once they knew a few beginning sounds. There was always a basket of blank books on the writing center in my kindergarten classroom to encourage student writing.

A tisket, a tasket, a little yellow basket. Writing was an inviting and fun task in my kindergarten and grade one classrooms, and I owe much of the popularity to a little yellow basket. You know, the inexpensive kind you buy on sale at the local discount bargain store. Teachers do spend lots of their own money on classroom embellishments and organizations, just as parents do. However, it's not the basket itself that provides the motivation to write; it's what inside that basket.

Tucked inside the basket was a stack of colorful blank booklets simply made with construction paper covers and plain newsprint, or scrap paper stapled together.

Sometimes I would cut pages and covers from paper grocery bags or old wallpaper. Great project for home, too. But you have to be willing to allow children to be messy and refrain from discouraging words such as, "This is how you should do it." There's nothing that sours a child's creative juices faster than an interfering, well-intentioned parent who wants the project to be "perfect."

Once, a parent sheepishly confided in me that she didn't want all that mess in her house, even though she recognized that her son was a true visionary. He could make something out of anything.

Some of my favorite pieces of saved student work are little books that students made for me, most created from blank books from that little yellow basket.

"The toolup

Written by Amber

One cold morning there was a toolup and it was groing in the gardin and somebude took it from the gardin it was the dog took it. The End"

The little book was in the shape of a tulip. The student had traced around a stencil of a tulip (yard sale find) on construction paper for her covers and the text was written in inventive spelling on a scrap paper page.

Although the basket overflowed with creativity and originality, the lasting intrinsic value of allowing students to create their own books and stories showed on their faces of these children when they shared their writing with an audience of their peers. This sharing was usually done from our Author's Chair. This was just a regular student chair with a hand-sewn black cover pulled down over the top with the words, "Author's Chair," glued on in red letters. After the student read his/her original story from the chair, other students would offer positive comments about the story, beginning with, "I like the way you..." Wide smiles of pleasure and self-confidence soon brimmed on the faces of the authors.

One such author wrote the following story when she was in the first grade:

"The farm

By Lee

At the farm I have a lamb.

At the farm I have pigs.

I miyt get a calf.

At the farm I have hens and a famly." She used inventive spelling for might and family.

Years after, while enrolled at the middle school, this student wrote, illustrated, and published her own story in the school's publishing center. Along with other students from the local middle school, she read the story to our class. She later presented the book to me with these words written on the dedication page.

"This book is dedicated to Mrs. Salway, my first grade teacher, who taught me the love of books and got me interested in writing them. Thank you, Mrs. Salway."

Now this former student is graduating from college.

Our classroom writing center was not an expensive school supply store purchase. It was a vintage (worn) table from an old school, the brick and mortar kind, adorned with a similar aged open book shelf propped along one long side of the back of the table. Both period pieces had three or four coats of brightly colored paint. Students chose their materials from the shelves and sat at the table to write during "free choice" time. (They thought the center was play.)

Local teachers in our district were fortunate to participate in a three-year writing grant project from the Bread Loaf School of English out of Middlebury College. We spent those three years reading, researching, writing, and discussing student writing samples with our colleagues. The knowledge I gained from those lively sessions held in the living room of our instructors was translated into classroom practice. Student writing is powerful. It can and should start even before children enter school. These are writings by kindergarten students.

"Mi dol" (My doll.)

BATRFL — BUTTERFLY

My BrtDay is tumor I AM GUNU havcac AND ic-crrm

One day I had the good fortune to observe the moment when a child actually made the leap from writing to reading. I felt my heart soaring, reaffirming that I had the best job in the world. It was as if I was witnessing the moment a monarch butterfly emerges from the chrysalis.

A first grade student with long thick golden braids was struggling with labeling her drawing of her pet cat. "I don't want to write all the letters, Mrs. S."

"That's all right, I will help you write a few and then if you have more to write, I will write the words for you."

After embellishing her illustrations, she wrote the words, "Mi cat ez blak", with my help. I remained at the same table, but I was seated directly opposite her helping another child, so I was able to observe what happened next.

She began to read what she had written, "Mi cat ez blak." Only this time she touched each set of letters as she read with her index finger. As she read the sentence over the second time, I noticed that she did not make the speech to print match. However, as she read the third time, her fingers touched the correct words one at a time as she said them.

Suddenly her head swung back quickly and her eyes lit up. Again and again she read her sentence. Then she exclaimed aloud, "Look. This says, My cat is black."

My heart was full. I was elated and felt like dancing around the room, however I did not want to diminish her reflective channeling.

The spark plug had caused ignition of the reading system illuminating a lifetime of literacy. It was the moment of impact. Words spouted forth inside my head:

"Do you hear me, world? This child has learned to read. For the rest of her life much of her success will depend upon what she just achieved."

It had been a marvelous sight to witness those actual moments when the writing/reading connection clicked. I left the table to go help other children. A little while later, I returned to see that she had added additional words all by herself.

"N MiMOMMYLIKzet" (And, my mommy likes it.)

A few days later, her mother told me that on that particular day, her little girl had come home overjoyed that she had learned how to write. (And read.) She had written all that evening illustrating a self portrait and labeling all the parts in inventive spelling.

On Friday of that week, this sunny lass walked up to me wearing a big grin.

"Mrs. S. Can I write all the time, now?" she requested.

I wanted to shout to the world, "This is why I teach."

I might not receive the pay of a CEO, but at that moment I felt as if I was the CEO of reading for this child. This same child announced to me the following week that she was changing her name to Star Princess.

Here is one of my favorite short stories written by a first grade student during the third quarter. The assignment was to write a story about her own mittens recorded on a mitten-shaped book.

"My Mitten

My mitten is warm. It is fluffy.

My mitten is rainbow colors.

My mom made it. This is a fiction story.

My mom does not knit."

What a joy to know that this child was able to take a risk in her writing—her voice and sense of humor woven throughout.

The following is a note I received from a grade one student once she was hit with the "writing bug."

"Mis Slway I Love Riting so much. I wot to do it so much. I wot to do it wan

Mrs. Salway, I love writing so much. I want to do it so much. I want to do it when

I am wriding. I Love Reet so moch. I wot to do it ivee sach of the day. It is fun.

I am riding. I love to read so much. I want to do it every second of the day."

Writing thoughts down on paper is a very powerful way for children to express innermost emotions and needs as long as their words are respected and not harshly judged.

It was a particularly tough day as a blond haired cherub, known to provide a challenge, continued to demonstrate inappropriate behavior towards his peers. (He called them names and made fun of their work.) As a result, he was placed in time out and lost free choice privileges. He was one of those who could melt your heart with his big blue eyes. He would look up at me with the most innocent gaze as if to suggest he could never do anything out of order. I resisted.

Later, while teaching a reading group at the reading table, he quietly walked up and slipped a piece of paper in front of me. It was a piece of manila lined writing paper from the writing center. He had obviously cut a large piece in two as the sides were uneven and one end torn. However, the message was clear.

"I am Sorry mrs. s that I Ben Bad. I will be god for Now on. Love S"

I still have this note, although yellowed from age, it remains a treasured keepsake.

Learning to read is the foundation upon which all else is built. So time spent listening to individual students reading aloud is precious, valuable time.

As a result, I had a rule that I was not to be disturbed at the Reading Table during reading group lessons, UNLESS someone was bleeding or sick. Every so often, this rule was challenged.

One winter morning I was sitting in my chair listening to a soft voice of a child reading aloud, when I sensed this small body leaning next to me. I also sensed there was no blood, so I did what any teacher would have done, I ignored this clingy non-bleeding, non-emergency, needy child. I turned away so I would not reinforce this unwanted behavior. "Miss Needy" now walked around me and put her face directly in front of mine.

"Are you sick?" I asked

"No," she whispered.

"Are you bleeding?"

"No"

"What is the matter?" I asked, thinking there must be something terribly wrong. "I can't find a white crayon," she whined.

I tried to refrain from overreacting in a manner not befitting a teacher. I showed restraint and whispered in her ear, "And where in this room do you think you could find a white crayon?" (I remained in control and didn't shout, "AND WHERE IN THIS ROOM COULD YOU FIND A WHITE CRAYON?")

"Oh, yeah, I forgot, over at the writing center."

The next morning I once again reiterated the difference between emergencies and non-emergencies and how I only had so much time to fit in all the reading groups. And, I once again asked the children to tell me what items they could readily access if materials are needed, such as extra crayons. In fact, there are always baskets and tins of extra crayons in a couple of locations. I also reminded the children that if they did have a problem needing my attention, they could write me a note and place it next to me and return to their seat.

The next day an unhappy child sauntered up to the table, lowered his head, and placed this note in front of me. I continued to listen to the child reading aloud. In a few minutes, after the unhappy child returned to his desk, I read the note. “evwe wun being men to Me.”

It was a joy to read some of the creative stories and journal entries written by my six and seven year old students. Sometimes it required unraveling detail with care and tactfulness. There's one heart-filled piece of writing that still resonates in my mind. It's a journal entry written just before Christmas. Most of the students were writing about their Christmas trees and what they wanted for Christmas. As I picked up the journal with the faded red cover, I turned to the new entry written by a little boy earlier in the day.

“All I wont for Christms is a home to liv in. We don't hav a home now. It will make my mom happy. We are livin with grammie.”

Another entry flooded my heart as I read:

“I jst wnt to lrn to red.” (I just want to learn to read.)

Sometimes the circumstances of others make our own worries and trials seem trivial. Children have never failed to touch my life in such ways that impact all that I do. Children constantly remind me of what's really important.

If I sing it, I'll remember it!

Chapter Thirteen
Embarrassing Moments

I could feel the warmth creep up my face and the palms of my hands becoming sweaty as I attempted to gift wrap the purchase. I sensed the customer's eyes watching every movement as I tied the ribbons creating the bow. Then, it happened as I feared it would. My hands started to tremble while my fingers curled the tiny strands. Quickly, I placed the package in a bag and handed it to the woman hoping she hadn't noticed.

Prior to stepping into the world of education, I held a part-time job as a sales clerk at a local gift shop. Often we gift-wrapped the purchases for our customers.

Why is this happening I cried to myself? I'd be perfectly fine one moment, then I'd feel this wave of fluttery anxiety roll through my body. Usually my hands would shake, sometimes so badly it was difficult to bring a teacup to my lips. It was terribly embarrassing if it happened at church while sipping juice in those tiny glasses during communion or at a social gathering. I'd often avoid drinking coffee in a small cup.

Later that day I called to make an appointment with my local physician.

"Blame it on one of your ancestors, probably a great-aunt. You have what's known as a familial tremor. It is known to run in families."

Throughout most of my teaching days it was not an issue, until I started to age.

Then, certain movements, especially writing, if attempted under any stress at all, would cause my hands to tremble. Even my husband commented that my head was shaking slightly.

"Oh, no, just like Katherine Hepburn."

Once I was asked to teach a reading/writing lesson behind the glass. This was done so viewers could sit on one side of the glass in one room and observe the teaching on the other side without distracting students.

Before listening to student's read, I introduced new vocabulary words. As I wrote each word on the large chart paper, students along with ten to twelve teachers on the other side of the glass watched.

I could feel the tension mounting. As the tension mounted, the fine motor control of my fingers diminished.

Maybe no one will notice, I thought hopefully.

I knew better. Children notice everything.

"Mrs. S, how come your letters are all wiggly and crooked?" a bright observant little boy asked. (Now, he chooses to notice letters.) Compounding the situation was knowing his acute observation had been amplified through the speakers and into the observation window for all to hear.

I was embarrassed almost to tears.

"They are, aren't they? Sometimes that happens."

The next day I sought help again from my physician.

"I teach penmanship," I wailed. "I can't have crooked letters interfering with my teaching. My trembling hands are interfering with my teaching ability."

I was relieved when he told me that many actors have the same issue and respond well to medication. What a relief.

Of course any humiliating incident rarely occurs in isolation. Those events always seem to occur with spectators en masse. Many parents and some teachers have tried to persuade children that they have eyes in the back of their heads, but in reality we miss a lot when our backs are turned, and some mischievous students take every advantage of that fact.

So to compensate, we often walk backwards as a behavior maintenance strategy, if we're walking in line.

This was not always a good idea.

Every year for Halloween, our entire school family dons our favorite costumes and walks downtown for our annual Halloween Parade. It is a grand affair for the entire town. Everybody—parents, grandparents, aunts, uncles, cousins—lines Main Street armed with cameras. Many business owners join the festivity, arriving in costumes to hand out goodies. The whole school gets into the act with our principal, teachers, ed techs, students, and parents dressing in their Halloween finery.

Usually I walked at the front of the line with two students, while parent volunteers took up positions in the middle and end of the line for the safety (ah, mischief patrol) of all the children. I was dressed in my Mary Poppins ensemble, complete with long skirt, blazer, gloves, straw hat, carpet bag, and umbrella. Even a sudden gust of wind adorned my whimsical presence by lifting the umbrella upward.

As I always did, I occasionally turned about-face to scan the behaviors of little ones behind me. As this Mary Poppins turned, however, her high button shoes caught in her long flowing skirt causing her to fall face-first toward the pavement. I quickly tried to balance myself but to no avail and I felt the hard thump, putting out my hand to break the fall.

There was Mary Poppins—facedown in the middle of Main Street with hundreds of people watching. Her bright-colored umbrella lay in the street, her white gloves covered in dirt. It was not a pretty sight. Trying to remain graceful, I untangled my feet from my skirt, and attempted to pick myself up with the help of a bystander. Red-faced and bruised in more ways than one, I managed to continue on my way.

"Oh, Mrs. S are you all right?" several of my students called to me.

"Oh yes, I'm fine. Don't worry."

That's what I said aloud. To myself, I'm thinking, "Oh

my god, how embarrassing. I just fell flat on my face, on Main Street, with half the town watching, while dressed as Mary Poppins."

What other professional would be able to recall this story for "all in a day's work?"

The next day a precocious child reminded me, "Mrs. S, don't walk backward. Remember what happened?"

Oh, I shall always remember. Not to mention is the fact I was wearing an ace bandage on my wrist due to a sprain caused by the fall.

Believe it or not, teachers don't sleep at school. I once had a child ask me if I did. Some students have been shocked to see me in the local grocery store. Now that's just fine if I happen to be buying spaghetti. But the minute I happen to have beer, wine, or sanitary napkins in my cart, suddenly there are three of four students appearing with their parents out of nowhere.

As I was shopping in a well-known department store thirty miles from home (safe), I picked out a couple of pair of underwear—one pair red, the other black. I had just placed the lingerie in my cart when I heard a familiar voice shouting, "Mom, look, it's my teacher."

As we exchanged pleasantries, I reached nonchalantly into the cart and flopped my handbag over the underwear in an attempt to hide the evidence. With a flushed face, I wondered if either had noticed the contents of my cart. Would this observant little person soon spread the scoop about the nature of his teacher's purchases to all his friends?

Or, would the astute parent relate?

Future teachers of America watch what and where you buy, for the little eyes of the world just might be watching.

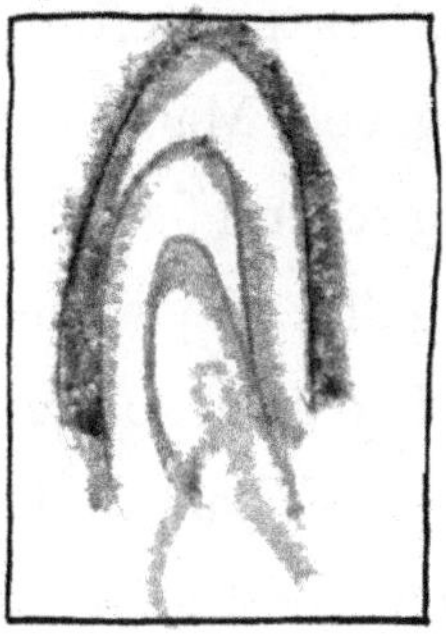

Chapter Fourteen
Guess What?

"Goooood morning, Mrs. S."

Every morning without fail, this bright-eyed little boy with a round face and big brown eyes would walk through the door and greet me with his cheeriest voice. His greeting always made me smile as I returned the gesture.

"Guess what, Mrs. S? Guess what I can do now?"

"Tell me, what can you do?"

"I can blow my nose the right way. I can blow the boogers out now instead of in."

As he delivered the news of his marvelous accomplishment, he leaned toward me and demonstrated.

"See, I can do it right now. I never could before. I have been practicing."

As I congratulated the proud lad on his newly acquired skill, I was captivated by his joy and I secretly chuckled about the incident the rest of the day.

Every parent and teacher goes into "be prepared"

mode when a child utters the words, "Guess what?"

It had been a long, cold Maine winter with major snowstorms dumping several feet of snow. Many forest creatures were having difficulty finding food supplies. As a result, several deer had been spotted near civilization, which in Maine is anyone's backyard. On this particular early spring day, one of my students shouted out, "Guess what? I see a moose eating the bushes."

Sure enough, as I ushered the class to the windows, we saw a baby moose nibbling on the shrubbery surrounding the school. He remained unaware of the number of faces pressed against window panes to get a closer look.

The moose continued to roam from bush to bush chewing on the evergreen tips. The next day several students wrote in their journals about the baby moose that came to school.

Another time the class and I were engaged in a handwriting lesson using the overhead projector to cast lines on the whiteboard. It was a warm, sunny late September afternoon with a slight breeze blowing through the opened window. Soon the silence was broken by a soft meowing.

Of course we all heard the pitiful cry and eighteen pairs of eyes looked over toward the screened window. Nothing. We went back to penmanship.

"Meow. Meow."

Once again the pleading calls of a feline wanting attention filled the room. This time two students quickly jumped out of their chairs to run to the window.

"We hear a cat, Mrs. S, but there's nothing there."

Curious, I walked over to look, scanning the grounds to see where the kitty was hiding.

Nothing.

We went back to work.

Then she spoke again. This time she revealed herself causing all of us to melt at the pathetic whimper and the tiny form. With her nose pressed against the screen, a small yellow kitten sat precariously on the window ledge peering into our classroom. Now, do you really think that those well-behaved students are going to sit there and just watch? Of course not. With words of caution from their teacher not to frighten the kitty, they walked closer to the window. However, having too many faces and bodies descend upon the area was too much for the curious kitty and she quickly scampered down and across the playground toward the apartments down the street. Penmanship lesson not completed that afternoon. Lesson about loving furry creatures accomplished.

One hot spring afternoon at the small elementary school where my career began, all the doors and windows were flung wide open, including the front door to the school. Unfortunately, this fresh air exposure would not be possible now with school doors locked. However, back in the early 1970s, a welcoming atmosphere was more of a concern than tight security.

The second grade teacher was reading aloud to her students when a neighbor dog decided to come in out of the heat. A large golden retriever sauntered up the steps of the old wooden yellow school. She immediately sniffed around in a circle, then settled down in the back of the classroom with her back leaned against the yellow wainscoted walls. She remained very quiet as if listening to the story. At first the students didn't even notice a dog at school as their eyes were on their teacher who was reading at the front of the room. Students and dog appeared most immersed in the story. Soon, the snickers erupted as the visitor's presence was discovered. Then, the curly haired intruder began to thump her tail in excitement to be surrounded by all the attention. Needless to say, her visit was temporary.

Guess what? Whether it's cries of a kitten, the sudden appearance of a moose or a dog, or the very first snowflakes, there is more that happens within the walls of a classroom that brings joy to a teacher and her students. Of course, one type of lesson was interrupted, but another about the marvels of nature was taught.

There is nothing more magical than watching a Monarch butterfly emerge from its chrysalis, except perhaps being witness to the actual spinning of the chrysalis. During the many years that we raised Monarchs in the classroom, only twice were the students and I able to catch this miraculous act of spinning.

Every September, as part of our science curriculum, all first graders were taught a unit on Life Cycles. As part of this study, I encouraged students and their parents to look for Monarch caterpillars to bring into the classroom along with the necessary supply of much needed milkweed leaves for nourishment. Most every year, children would carry their mayonnaise jars with holes poked in the lids excitedly to school. The jars would contain one or two fat, green/yellow caterpillars and a supply of milkweed leaves. Every morning and several times during the day students would check the size of the caterpillars. One morning a little girl went over to her jar only to discover that the two caterpillars had escaped.

"Guess what, Mrs. S. My caterpillars got out. Where can they be?"

We searched the classroom looking for the two escape artists but were unable to locate the creatures. The following week as I picked up the yellow plastic basket housing all our journals, a student called out in alarm, "Look out, Mrs. S. There's a chrysalis on the basket. You almost have your hand on it."

The Journal Basket had been sitting on the counter next to the jar containing the caterpillars. One of them must have crawled out and spun its cocoon beneath the plastic rim of the basket. We had to carefully place the entire basket on top of the file cabinet where all could witness the transformation. For fourteen days we watched the tiny green chrysalis with its gold dots change from green to black.

As the tiny structure became more translucent, getter darker and darker, students were not able to concentrate on their work as they knew at any moment the butterfly might emerge. All eyes, including mine, kept glancing at the one-inch-long marvel.

Then, just minutes after returning to the room from outside recess, the grand show began.

"Guess what? I think it's happening. Look." a student shouted. "It's wiggling. It's wiggling. I think she's coming out."

We all gathered around to watch the entrance of our butterfly into the world. Quietly, we stood in awe as the black and orange wings broke through. She hung there twirling slightly. Then, the wings dropped down again to the loud oohs and ahhhs from the children. She was drying her wings.

"Is it a girl or a boy, Mrs. S? Does it have the black spots?"

We had learned that the male butterflies have a black spot on each of its hind wings. After the wings were dry and the large wings unfurled, we could plainly see that this butterfly was a girl. Carefully, I moved the butterfly into a special butterfly box with nectar and flowers for the remainder of the day. The next morning, the whole class walked outside to bid farewell to our new friend. I reached inside the box to allow the butterfly to crawl onto my outstretched finger. Several students also wanted to hold the butterfly. They giggled as the thin claws tickled little fingers. Suddenly, the orange/black/white butterfly flitted from the finger and rose up into the bright blue sky head-ing south, to the waves and "good-byes" from happy/sad children.

That image and joy is forever etched in the minds and hearts of students and their teacher.

Another classroom science project the students and I pursued was the year long observation of a tree near the schoolyard. Since seasons in Maine are clearly defined by the obvious seasonal changes, it's always a fun way of teaching the cycle.

During the first week of school we went outside, chose our tree, and studied its formation. The students noticed that the tree was covered with bright green leaves. These observations, along with an illustration, were recorded by students in a special My Tree Observation booklet.

Again, in the fall, we observed, recorded and illustrated the now colorful leaves, some falling to the ground. During the winter, students recorded the tree with its bare branches.

Then, it happened. We had just returned to school from our April vacation.

"Guess what? Oh no. You are going to be very upset Mrs. S. Our tree is gone."

"What do you mean, our tree is gone?" I asked.

I followed my bewildered students to the large classroom windows overlooking the playground. Sure enough, the tree was gone. Not a trace. It had been cut down and branches hauled away. Upon investigation with the maintenance crew, we learned that the tree was showing signs of poor health and felt for safety reasons it should be removed from the playground. Of course, no one knew the tree was part of a science project.

Anyway, we made the most of a sad situation. On the last page of their Tree Observation Journal, students wrote, "Our tree was cut down."

It was a week before Christmas and we were busily making gifts for parents. More precisely, we made gingerbread cookie ornaments. After they were baked and ribbon strung through the hole, I placed the tree and star shaped ornaments outside on the picnic table where I could safely spray them with a protective coating. I placed them outside on the table in the morning, carefully counting to be sure every student had a completed project. After lunch, I returned to the table to retrieve the dried decorations. However, as I delivered the aroma-filled ornaments to students, two students were missing their creative projects.

"Where is mine, Mrs. S?"

I had counted when I placed the trays outside so I knew there were eighteen.

We all counted again. There were only sixteen cookies.

I assured the children that the missing cookies must have fallen off the table and we would be sure to find them.

But, we didn't.

Now, our playground has resident crows—three to be

exact. Crows are such scavengers and are known to descend upon the playground directly after recess to clean up.

That's what they did. They cleaned up on gingerbread cookies sprayed with polyurethane.

A few weeks later as a custodian was retrieving a ball that had landed on the roof, she noticed two broken gingerbread cookies tied with bows nestled in a crack on the roof. Ever since we looked at those crows wondering if they all had digestion issues.

As for the two missing cookies? We made new ones.

Sometimes, I was the person exclaiming, "Guess what?"

The incident happened one spring day as I was leaving school for the drive home. It had been rainy all afternoon. The sun broke through revealing a bright blue sky as I walked across the parking lot. Entering my car, I glanced up. There in the sky over the roof of our elementary school was a magnificent rainbow. The colors were radiant. I reached inside my purse for my camera to capture this miracle of nature. As I snapped the picture I pondered how exciting it would be to share this spectacle with the children in the morning.

The following morning, after the routine chores were completed, the flag saluted and daily message read, we gathered around the easel. I sat in my large rocking chair, a nice touch for teachers that awaited us when the new addition was completed. After we read our poems together, students shared their news and I waited my turn to share mine.

"Boys and girl, guess what I saw last night?" I began. "I saw a beautiful rainbow in the sky over our school. Did anyone else see it?" I inquired.

Before anyone could answer, a student raised his hand. I was shocked at his response.

"Mrs. S, you know rainbows are NOT real. They are only in books."

"You have never seen a real rainbow?" I asked.

"Well, I've seen them in books," he responded as other students tried to reassure him that his teacher was indeed telling him the truth, that rainbows were real.

I quickly remembered the photo I'd taken and showed it to him.

"I've never seen one." he replied.

"One of these days you will see one and you'll be amazed. I hope you see a rainbow soon. Look up in the sky after it's rained and the sun is shining. You are likely to see a rainbow." I said reassuringly. I felt so sad that in the seven years of his young life he had yet to witness the miracle of seeing a rainbow.

Thus began an exploration into what conditions cause the formation of rainbows. We read non-fictional accounts about rainbows in our study of light. I only hoped that he would soon experience the thrill of seeing a real rainbow.

Life is full of surprises, some good, some not so good. In the world of children, animals, and nature, there will be many surprises. But it's important to celebrate those simple daily joys and to make the most of those teachable moments.

Reading aloud to my students, was one of the greatest joys of teaching.

Chapter Fifteen
Sing It. Act It.

One Halloween long ago, to my astonishment, my mother dressed as a cat and went trick-or-treating by herself to the home of our elderly neighbors. I recall coming home from a Halloween party and finding her sitting at our kitchen table complete with black tights, tail, and a big grin between her whiskered mask. My sisters and I were unaccustomed to seeing my mom in a costume, and we were thrilled with her sense of playfulness. Usually my mom displayed a more serious side. This escapade gave us a glimpse into another side of my mom and we loved it. We never forgot it and neither did her surprised neighbors.

That sense of frivolity and ability to make children laugh is important in the home and in the classroom. Although it's important to maintain discipline and management, there are ways to liven up the delivery. Kids love the unusual throw-them-off-guard approaches.

Once when my own kids were teens, they were flopped

in front of the television on a hot summer day while I was out weeding the garden and picking berries. So I proceeded to do some dramatic acting to enlist their help outside without the usual nagging, especially since they liked to eat the sweet berries. I flung myself in front of the TV set, arms waving over my head and announced in my best TV announcer voice, "This is your mother speaking. I interrupt this program to bring you a special announcement. There are weeds in the garden that need to be pulled and delicious berries that need picking and this mother needs your help."

Reaching behind me, I turned off the television. Staring me in the face were two stunned teens, who quickly roared in laughter.

"Yes mom, we got the message. We'll be out to help you."

One of my favorite ways to attract student attention after usual attempts had failed, is the use of foreign languages. Yes, I mean foreign, even to me. Now I don't speak any foreign language fluently, but I can sure make up my own version on the spot if needed. And there are times when we have to diversify our deliveries.

On a cold winter day prior to Christmas break, when student heads were full of sugar plums and their attention span was nonexistent, I found myself several times addressing the class to no avail. So foreign language dribbled out of my tongue with flowery loud resonance. I stood on a chair and proceeded to spout every word in French, Spanish, Italian, and many words that were not real words at all. The students didn't know the difference. It was all in the delivery.

Oh, yes, I got their attention all right. As the strange sounding words came forth, the students stopped their chatting and stared at me with their mouths open. They instantly became silent. (In the meantime, I'm laughing on the inside. Teachers do that often, you know.) I'm congratulating myself, "It worked. It worked. They are so gullible."

Another time I wanted to teach my first grade students about the difference in reading aloud when there was an exclamation mark at the end of a sentence. So I read a sentence normally, then climbed up on the table and shouted the line.

"I sure hope the principal doesn't come in and see you standing on the table, Mrs. S. You could get into trouble."

I made a point, however, as their reading expression improved dramatically. A little girl showed me her journal the next morning in which she had added several exclamation marks.

"See, all these marks I added, Mrs. S? It says, 'I was so scared!'"

Unfortunately there was a downside to that overzealous approach. Another child proceeded to write her sentence, but filled the remainder of the page with dozens of exclamation marks. Thus, began a new lesson in "appropriate use of punctuation."

As an introduction to one of our reading books, I dressed up as the main character. While the students were outside for recess, I put on the costume and gathered the props. Just before the students were arriving back inside the classroom, I hid in the bathroom. As was the routine after morning recess, students brought their chairs to the story circle near the easel awaiting me to read the story.

"Where is Mrs. S? She isn't here."

I began to sing operatic notes loudly from inside the bathroom as I flung open the door.

To squeals of delight, the children recognized my character with the bedroom slippers and listened intently as I introduced myself before reading aloud. Just recently I had a parent remind me that she had walked into my room to witness that transformation many years ago. Neither she nor her daughter had forgotten the moment.

Sing it and I'll remember it better.

From learning to sing the ABC song, to learning the parts of the human body, to reciting the preamble to the Constitution, new material becomes easier to remember if put to a tune and sung over and over again. Research supports this theory with new understanding of brain development. As a result, we have sung our way through many areas of the curriculum.

One November morning while observing students drawing their own maps and adding a key and detail, I heard someone singing.

"Mrs. S, she is singing and it's bothering me."

As I leaned down to whisper for the little girl to sing in her head, she said to me, "But I can remember what to do if I sing the How to Make a Map Song. I can't remember all the parts so I have to keep singing to help me remember what else to put on my map."

Another time a 4th grader, a former student of mine, was serving as a mentor in the classroom and remarked, "I will always remember how to say happy birthday in Spanish because we used to sing the song in English and Spanish when we were in first grade."

"Feliz Cuplianos."

One of the biggest surprises was a high school senior visiting the classroom and remarking, "Do you know I still remember the words to our "Line up Song" and sometimes I start singing it in the girl's locker room."

"Hands at your sides. Eyes on me. Ready to walk down the hall quietly. If you're not quiet and act politely, you will owe me."

Many years ago, I was working as an aide in a small rural school building with just three grades. The kindergarten teacher had an old upright piano in one corner of the classroom. Whenever, she wanted the attention of the whole class, she would go over to the piano and play a short tune. It was a joy to watch those twenty-five students stop what they were doing and focus on their teacher from the musical cue.

While sitting with a parent during a parent-teacher conference, she looked at me and asked with a puzzled look, "Do you mind if I ask you a question? What's this I hear about a magic red button on the floor? My son tells me all the time that you step on a red button on the floor to get the students to pay attention. I looked when I came in and I didn't see one. Is that true?"

We both laughed as I revealed the fact that the magic red button was only pretend. It was just a certain spot on the floor at the front of the classroom, but when I announced to the class every morning that I was stepping on the magic red button, everyone became quiet. Children love make-believe.

During the first few weeks of school in September, first grade students tire easily from the transition from summer lazy days to busier school days. Often, I would pretend to sprinkle sand on them (from the Sandman) for calming, while inviting them to lay their heads on their desks. Sometimes, I'd read. Sometimes, I'd play music. On this particular day, I sang. Now, I possess nothing more than your average voice when it comes to crooning, but in the classroom it helps to be able to sing a little. In fact, we sang all the time. We sang the rules. We sang to clean up. We sang to quiet down. We sang to listen to the teacher. I would often invent songs on the spot to emphasize a subject.

So on this particular day, I began to sing a book I'd just bought at a yard sale, a patriotic book titled, *This Land is My Land*. I walked around the room softly singing to the children. My back was turned away and I did not notice my principal walk into the room to observe how the students were adjusting. I almost lost my composure when I realized she was watching and listening but I couldn't stop now. So I continued ever so self-conscious of my aging crackling voice.

Once I dressed as a giant green leprechaun for St. Patrick's Day. Looking back, I question my sanity. I was working as a teacher's aide/secretary and joined the whole school celebration. All three classes gathered in the large kindergarten classroom to listen to Irish stories read by a retired teacher, and to make green pudding. I had the job of skipping around in my green velveteen pantsuit with a green cap carrying a black bucket containing vanilla wafer "gold" that I delivered to waiting children. As everyone took turns adding the ingredients and beating the pudding, the wobbly old table gave way.

Too many items on the table along with too many children leaning on the old green table caused it to tip over spilling green pudding everywhere. Luckily all was not lost and at least all were treated to wafers from the giant green leprechaun.

Sometimes the actions are unplanned. One February, we had just finished reading a story about Abe Lincoln. One of my kindergarten students was returning from a trip down the hall to use the boys' room. As he entered the room, he was gushing with excitement. He could not exit the words fast enough.

"He's here. He's in the hallway. I saw Abe Lincoln in the hall. I really did. Go look. He walked into a classroom."

I went to the door to investigate just in time to see the tall, bearded gentleman enter the classroom across the hall. He was an elementary supervisor for student teachers from the University of Maine at Farmington here to check in with a student teacher. He did indeed look just like Abe Lincoln.

That child talked about that encounter for the remainder of the school year.

Reading aloud to my own children at bedtime was one of the greatest joys of parenting.

Reading aloud to my students at story time was one of the greatest joys of teaching. There are certain books that have to be read with just the right delivery. In order to make the story and characters come alive it depends on our voices and the theatrical embellishments we portray. Yes, sometimes it's the use of props— from pebbles, to caps, to bells or aprons. Whatever you use, will create a magical atmosphere to enrich the words of the story and pull your readers into the action and emotions on the pages.

Do what you need to do. Use whatever your imagination allows. The elements of surprise and humor can make a huge impact on your ability to make a point or get attention in your living room or classroom. And it doesn't cost money. The results are treasured memories.

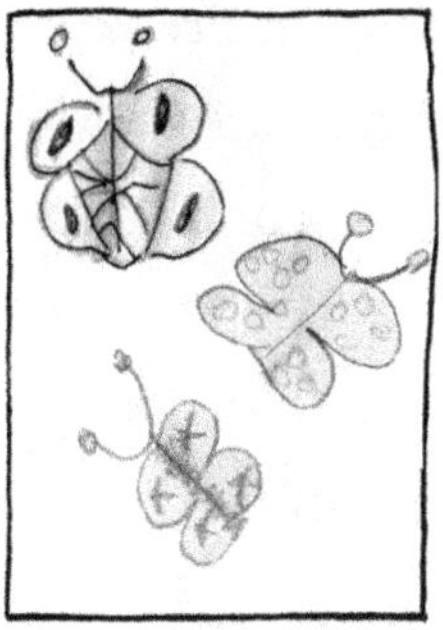

Chapter Sixteen
Attention

Babies do it. Toddlers do it. Children of all ages do it. Even adults do it. Yes, our pets do it.

Let's face it. Everyone likes a little attention, some more than others. We've witnessed all kinds of antics from infants to aged men and women, doing their best to draw attention to themselves, whether it's fussing, or wearing crazy attire or hairstyles. A wise veteran teacher once warned me about "negative attention" behaviors. She cautioned, "Don't fall into the trap of reinforcing a child's attempt to receive negative attention. For some children, negative attention is better than no attention at all. It only takes one time for a child to receive attention for an inappropriate behavior, and the next time, he/she will try again, again, and again. As long as a child keeps receiving some form of attention for that misbehavior then he will wear you down with even more attempts. If a temper tantrum works the first time to get a toy in a store, believe me, another tantrum will occur. Prepare to be worn down."

I was as guilty as anyone. And it was my big yellow cat, Mittens, who wore me down. Unfortunately, she did it in the middle of the night when I was desperate for sleep and inefficient at making sane decisions. Making one poor decision, namely in the form of food, at three in the morning, was only the beginning. IT ONLY TAKES ONE TIME AND THEY DON'T FORGET. It took a long time to undo her midnight cravings.

Pets continue a behavior when it is rewarded and stop a behavior when it is ignored. There are always exceptions, of course.

As a parent, I was familiar with how easily babies learn to cry when they want to be picked up and held. They are so intelligent at such an early age. However, as that baby gets older, he or she uses more sophisticated measures to gain the desired outcome. When toddlers receive attention for appropriate behaviors, we call it positive attention. When they display inappropriate behaviors and receive attention, we call it negative attention.

We have all been victims of a young child's savvy, clever displays, usually in a crowed place with many witnesses to observe how we will react. Children are so clever. Of course they will throw a tantrum in the middle of the mall where all the shoppers are watching, in an effort to get a desired toy. The gawking onlookers will be watching and observing to see how you react, secretly grateful that the child is not their child. The child in the meantime knows exactly how to get his/her own way by screaming and throwing themselves onto the floor.

"Here you go. Okay, you can have the toy, but only this time. Stop crying, please," coaxes the flustered, irritated, totally embarrassed parent.

There. That was easy. Crisis averted. Child now wears a big smile and carries a new toy. Screaming stops. Parent is relieved that the attention is no longer on them and can resume the shopping. Onlookers are no longer staring. The day is saved.

But you will pay for more than a toy. You might pay for the rest of your life.

In the middle of the mall, the child outmaneuvered the parent.

In the middle of the night, my cat outsmarted me.

Do you think it might have been wiser to scoop up the theatrical but hysterical cherub and usher him or her out the door to the parking lot while repeating, "I said no, and you are not having a toy. That's what I meant. There will be no toy today."

In a classroom, those attempts at gaining negative attention can affect an entire classroom.

I was taught that in order to diminish an undesirable behavior, you ignore it (unless, of course, the behavior is dangerous to the child or someone else).

One day, while a parent volunteer was helping a student with unfinished work in my classroom, I was leading the rest of the class in the reading of our morning message. As

I pointed to the words on the white board, a student in the back row began rolling crayons down his desk, first one then another. Soon, another child started copying the same crayon contest on his desk. I ignored them both at first, not wanting to give them the attention they were seeking, however, other students were beginning to pay more attention to the crayon culprits than to me.

Seizing the moment, I redirected my attention to a couple of students on the other side of the room who were sitting quietly while paying attention.

"Wow, just look at how well you two are paying attention. Thank you so much. You both are showing me model student behavior, aren't they boys and girls? I appreciate that."

Quick as a wink, one of the crayon duo tossed his crayons into his desk, folded his hands, and placed them quietly on his desk. The other lad followed and soon his crayons were inside the desk.

Well, I thought the parent volunteer was going to fall out of her chair as she witnessed the antics.

"I couldn't believe how you managed to correct those two without a word spoken to them. It was like magic." she whispered to me after.

Sometimes though, just when we think we are so smart, a student enlightens and educates us with a lesson and we're the ones outsmarted.

One afternoon, in the middle of a math lesson, a little boy with sparkling blue eyes began tipping his chair back.

I ignored it. With his eyes directly on mine, he moved his chair back and tipped it again to be sure I had seen his maneuver.

Again, I ignored the teetering. At least ten minutes passed with him tipping, tipping, and tipping, and me ignoring, ignoring, ignoring. I was getting concerned that he would fall over and bump his head.

As predicted, other students were distracted from the math to sneak glances at the inappropriate chair balance show. I had to do something.

With my eyes focused on a child sitting appropriately, I announced, "Thank you K— for sitting so nicely during the math lesson."

"I know what you're doing, Mrs. S. You're trying to change my behavior," the tipper artist shouted across the room, raising his voice to be sure I heard his announcement.

Needless to say the caper cost him minutes in "time out" while others were at play, followed by a discussion with him about making good choices.

One morning, while taking the hot lunch count, a little person began to tap his pencil on top of his desk. I ignored it. Again and again he tapped. Again and again I ignored. Soon, I had enough, so without saying a word I quietly leaned over and took the pencil away. You guessed it. He quickly took another pencil from his desk and began tapping away again. This time, I went to the board and wrote five minutes on the board. The tapping stopped. Tapping

Tim knew that now he owed me "time out."

Later on that same day, while I was leading a reading group and students were working at their seats or at centers, the room was silent except for the voice of the student reading aloud.

"Tap, tap, tap."

With eyes as big as saucers, Tapping Tim looked around the room to see who was watching. Everyone ignored him. Now keep in mind, we had previously had class discussions about the need to ignore attention getting behaviors.

Children will continue a behavior when it is rewarded and stop a behavior when it is ignored.

I kept my eyes on the reading book, but could observe out of the corner of my eye. Soon the little girl sitting across from Tapping Tim stands up, walks over to his desk, takes the pencil out of his hand and slams it down onto his desk. With her hands on her hips, looking him straight in the eye, she whispered loudly, "Stop that."

"Okay," he said in a weak voice, gazing at her in astonishment.

Now ordinarily I don't commend students being in charge of another's behavior, but in this case I had to chuckle because it worked. You never know. Sometimes your peers, particularly if that peer happens to be a cute little brown-eyed girl, have a powerful effect.

What worked best in the end to diminish Tapping Tim's tapping was the sprinkling of large doses of positive attention throughout the day when he was showing me any behavior that was appropriate. A home/school contract reinforced those positive behaviors as well.

I tell you these stories for two reasons. First of all, to warn you of the slippery slope of attention-getting maneuvers. Secondly, to give you a glimpse into how long some days can be.

Remember, children will continue a behavior when it is rewarded and stop a behavior when it is ignored. Remember also, that sometimes all attempts fail. There are no magic words. We just keep trying to help kids.

At a retirement gathering for a seasoned educator, he whispered into my ear, "I can't believe the decline in behaviors of children since the old days. You know, since the whole fear of child abuse brought an end to spanking, some parents don't discipline their children at all."

Shaking his head, he added, "I watch some young parents sit idly by not stopping their rude, bullying aggressive child from hurting another child."

We know his observations are correct. However, times have changed.

It's not the old days. Times and parenting, along with increasing demands on families, have placed more stress on working mothers and fathers, single parents, grandparents, and caregivers.

I believe part of the success in meeting the academic and emotional needs of today's students is the collaboration between school and home. We need to work in cahoots with each other.

A parent once requested that I email him if and when his child misbehaved. He emphasized that he wanted his child to know that he and I were in "cahoots" for the child's best interest. I chuckled at his wording but appreciated his support.

One of the most challenging issues for me as a classroom teacher was addressing attention seeking behaviors and inappropriate behaviors of a student with his or her parents. None of us want to hear that OUR child is capable of doing wrong. Even more difficult, is how to present the scenario that perhaps the parents are contributing to those behaviors by unknowingly rewarding poor behaviors.

I would ask myself, "How do I tactfully tell a parent that by repeatedly giving in to the child's whining, cries, and temper tantrums, they are teaching that child to behave badly?"

Children are smart. Children are clever. They learn quickly how to be "at the controls" and manipulate parents and teachers. Parents of America must take back control and not be afraid to parent.

Chapter Seventeen
Patriotism

Covered with chicken pox and wearing his flannel baseball-striped pajamas, our five-year-old son stood in the center of his bed with one hand over his heart and the other holding a popsicle. He stood there unaware that I was gazing at this precious moment. Tears of joy trickled down my cheek as I watched while he stood at attention during the playing of our national anthem prior to the beginning of the Red Sox baseball game broadcasting on the bedside radio.

Perhaps this was not exactly an act of patriotism, but my son did know to stand during the national anthem. It didn't matter that he was standing up on his bed.

Patriotism was strong in our classroom. Every day in kindergarten a child would hold the American flag while we recited the "Pledge of Allegiance." Words to the "Pledge" were printed above the flag to help children establish the speech to print match as they recited the words. Patriotism is more than waving a flag and reciting the "Pledge of Allegiance," however. The word patriotism itself stirs up controversy about many interpretations, political views, and definitions depending on the partisan stance on the current political debate.

But in a child's world, seeds of compassion for one's country and the freedoms we hold can be planted early in life. "Let patriotism bloom before the blight of wars and politics withers the buds of citizenship and pride," I once read.

"I got to hold the flag this week," a child would proudly tell his/her parents.

Holding the flag was one of our classroom jobs in which students participated to help teach citizenship and classroom responsibilities. Holding the flag was more than a job, however. It was an activity that taught children the importance of our freedoms by their daily engagement.

Standing and saluting the flag, of course, is controversial. I stand proudly on my conviction that children learn by doing. There were many moments, however, when the morning ritual was repeated for one reason or another. Usually some mischievous one would decide to speed up the delivery by loudly racing through the words, throwing off the entire class. He or she would smugly observe the reactions from annoyed classmates while gaining attention from how quickly the pledge was recited. His teacher was not amused.

Enter teachable moment. Enter lesson on respect.

Then, there was the daily check to be sure each child was using the "right" hand over their heart. Many times, I'd witness a child switch to the incorrect hand by glancing around the room at placement of hands. Young students often have difficulty with left/right directionality. The puzzle for developing children is compounded upon facing another child whereby he/she feels that the hand is not on the same side. So they switch, thinking their hand should be on the same side.

Many times, I'd face the same direction. I'd place my right hand over my heart, then turn to face them.

"Did my hand move?" I'd ask. Several times, I'd repeat the turn and face them, changing positions so they could actually see that when two students are facing one another, the right hands will be opposite one another.

Understanding the words to the "Pledge of Allegiance" is another challenge for young children. Students have been confusing the pronunciation of those words since long before I was in school. There have been numerous and humorous renditions written about misinterpretations. Most teachers of young children have heard every version for themselves.

One little girl wrote about reciting the "Pledge of Allegiance" in her daily journal:

"I lik sain the pleg. It gos. I plej a lee gents to the flag of the you nited stats of ameika.and to the wepubk for Rich ed stans 1nashn, undr god indeevis apple wth lib partee and jus tess for al."

During our annual studying of symbols of the United States in first grade, we learned more about the story behind our first flag, Uncle Sam, the bald eagle, and the Statue of

Liberty. The entire grade one population once presented an assembly on the theme of our patriotic symbols. Wearing red, white, and blue, all seventy-two students carried flags, led the whole school in the "Pledge," recited poems and sang patriotic songs. Immersed in involvement through movements and songs along with other senses, students learn about social studies by actively connecting.

We participated in Election Day activities by casting votes in the classroom and walking to the polls to watch townspeople vote. In later years voting was held in the gym of our school enabling us to quietly watch the whole process. Red, white, and blue balloons would adorn our voting booth as every student in the school voted in a mock election for president.

One year during the gubernatorial race in Maine, Angus King was one of the candidates. The morning after the election, a freckled-faced little girl walked through the doorway to our kindergarten classroom and announced, "Did you hear? The King won."

Another time, along with classroom teachers, I helped escort a group of first and second graders on a short walk to the polling place just down the street from the small elementary school. One of our teachers was married to a republican member of the Maine Legislature. She, of course, was a supporter of the republican candidate for President and wore her elephant necklace that day. The children didn't know the meaning of it. As we approached the school on the return trip, a group of students began to chant, "We want Jimmy. We want Jimmy," referring to the Democratic candidate, Jimmy Carter.

There is nothing more beautiful than a group of young children singing "America the Beautiful" or "America."

As I walked my young kindergarten students down the hall to art class, we passed by the first grade classroom where the teacher began every morning of her thirty-plus years of teaching with the singing of "God Bless America." That classroom would eventually become my first grade classroom upon "Mother Superior's" retirement. The nick-name was given to this veteran teacher out of respect and affection. This was not a Catholic school, either. She had taught so long and could vividly recall incidents, students, and history of unsuccessful educational practices, and details of past administrations. She could whip out her views and comments with candor and whit, never mincing words. She even had her own chair in the teacher's room, labeled "Mother Superior."

Thou did not sit in her chair.

One of the toughest days of teaching was September 11, 2001. It was a beautiful clear day with bright blue skies. As I walked my first grade students past the glass walls of the main office, I noticed the secretary and principal gathered around a TV set in the principal's office.

The pensive looks on their faces told me something troublesome had happened in the news. After delivering my students to physical education class I returned to the office where I found others with concerned, anguished faces.

A plane had flown into the World Trade Center. That's all I knew at first, along with the rest of the world. How did that happen? It must have been a horrible accident, we thought. A short time later I walked down again to the office to hear that another plane had hit the Pentagon.

The news was sickening. Our country had been attacked by terrorists. The scenes on the television became more and more horrible as the towers began to crumble. As the smoky images and blood-stained faces filled the screen, fears rose inside me and those around me.

Our immediate thoughts were of the safety of our students in our own building. Would there be air strikes? Would the students be safe? What about our own families? The phones began to ring. What were we to do? How do we handle this type of news with very young students?

Our principal called a special meeting for all staff at noon to address the issue. In the meantime, we tried to carry on, not wanting to cause any undo alarm until we knew the circumstances. Part of me wanted to race home and call my own children and grandchildren. I wanted to tell them I loved them. I wanted to hug them. Instead, members of the staff of our school did an incredible job keeping in control. It was decided that a letter would go home to parents granting them the decision as to how and what to explain the world situation.

The following day, we made flags—all kinds of flags. Some students painted large flags at the easel. Other students colored, cut, and glued little flags onto straw holders. One little girl wrote a story about our flag in her journal. The class was unusually calm and peaceful that day.

"I need a hug, Mrs. S."

I heard this request for reassurance from several of my young students many times during the days following the attack. I felt however, that parents had provided extra doses of hugs and kisses along with conveyance of comforting words.

Once in a while a child would comment on the towers falling down. The most important part of that day was reassuring the children of their safety at our school. I felt fear rise inside me as I'd never felt before.

The lives of my students and mine would never be the same again.

There were immediate changes in the security of our school.

No longer did we teach with our doors open. No longer did we prop the outside entry doors open to allow fresh air or stray dogs to stream through. All staff wore keys to the entry doors to enter during outside recess.

Any person entering the building was required to sign in at the office. Our secretary once ran down the hallway to confront a stranger who passed by quickly without checking in and receiving the necessary visitor badge. How sad that every new face entering our school was now instantly viewed as a potential threat. We had to be alert for the safety of our students.

During the days and weeks following 9/11, many of

the students shared their concerns through journal entries and illustrations. Perhaps compounding fears in our small picturesque town in the western hills of Maine was learning that the hijackers boarded the plane in Maine before arriving in Boston. That news jarred teachers and parents. That news jarred our children.

"Mrs. S., did you know that those bad men were in our state? How could they do that? Why would they hurt all those people?"

One of my favorite memories of flag holding experiences will forever linger in my heart. It happened while I was teaching junior kindergarten. One of my chronologically very young students had difficulty with social interactions with his peers. He remained on the sidelines simply observing the rest of us for several weeks. Slowly, as trust in me and his peers increased, so did his participation in activities.

When it came his turn to hold the flag, I invited him to come to the front of the class as he'd observed his classmates. At first he'd always decline, however the invitation was always presented.

One day, a giant step was made. Actually they were a series of small footsteps from one side of the room to the front of the classroom. However, those steps were huge strides in self-confidence.

"Would you like to hold the flag today? Gerry is absent."

No response. As I prepared to ask another child, I turned around to see him slip out of his chair and walk, not crawl, past the tables to the center of the room. Ever so slowly, he took each step carefully.

For you see his eyes were closed, and remained partly closed throughout the recitation. I could just barely see a glimpse of him sneaking a peek from under his long black eyelashes.

Tears filled my eyes as I witnessed this milestone in this child's life.

Soon after, he began to verbalize more as well as engage in more activities.

"Oh, mother," he called out to me one day.

Another time, after returning to the classroom from a trip to the rest room, he noticed that we'd proceeded to the "weather report" portion of our morning opening lessons.

"You didn't do the flag?" he asked in a concerned voice.

"No, we waited for you."

The broad smile that emerged on that precious face warmed my soul. This child taught me a valuable lesson in how trust and tiny increments of self-esteem boosters can foster positive outcomes.

This was more than a lesson in patriotism. This was more than holding the flag. This was validation of the worth of a child. When this child was graduating from high school, he walked into my classroom carrying a bouquet of flowers and a heartfelt note.

Celebrate the best in nature.

Chapter Eighteen
Grief

The old black rotary dial phone rang early that morning. Usually, the call would be a parent alerting the school that a child was sick and would be absent from school that day. On the other end of the line, a parent began to sob as she informed me that her young son would be late to school because his cat had just been run over in front of their house.

"Would it be all right if he brought in the cat's collar to school, as he was comforted by holding it?"

Every parent, every teacher, sooner or later is faced with tragedy in a school family, whether it be a pet, a grandparent, a parent, sibling, aunt or uncle. You can be sure it will happen when you least expect it. However, because of the bombardment of scenes on television in which children are often exposed to deaths, their only experience with the real act of grieving happens in their own families, school, community, or world tragedies. It's real. Children feel the raw emotions and the sting of tears and broken hearts.

There's a favorite book of mine that I read every year to my class. It's an emotional story about losing a pet. Usually I am unable to read it aloud without tearing up. At first, I used to be embarrassed by my tears. Then, I began relating to students prior to reading that many stories are so well written that the story brings us to tears as they remind us of our own experiences.

"I might cry when I read this, but please don't be upset."

As I approached the end of the book and nearing the difficult section to read, I noticed some of the children sitting on the floor close to me were tilting their heads, checking my eyes. The tears flowed as I sobbed through the blurry words.

Many of the children rose to their feet and threw their arms around me. A couple of children had tears as well. I never stopped reading that story.

For years I always had a classroom pet, usually a furry, squeaky guinea pig. One, named Butterscotch, I had for a long time. Another was named Gus.

Gus never seemed to be as strong as other guinea pigs. He was the runt of the litter. Early one morning upon arrival, I spoke to him as I usually did while reaching to give him a scratch on his little black head. I was shocked to see him lying on the shavings gasping for breath. Immediately, I rushed to the phone to call my vet. I was told to bring him right down, only a mile away. I called the office to ask for someone to cover my classroom until I returned. Wrapping Gus in his miniature fleece blanket, I snuggled him close and ran to my car.

The prognosis was not good. Gus had two overgrown teeth that were preventing his mouth from closing correctly, but there was hope that he could survive. I returned to the classroom to give an update to the concerned group.

Late in the day I received a call from the vet, however, informing me that Gus did not make it. Everything had been done for him but he was just too weak.

We gathered on the rug where I broke the news. We cried. We talked. We remembered all the things we liked about our little pet. We talked about how we felt sad.

The conversation grew to individual accounts of other deaths students had experienced in their young lives and how they had been affected. I tried to reassure the children that it was normal to feel sad and to cry when someone we love dies. After the students left on the busses, the room was silent. It had been a long emotion-filled day.

During the next day there were several conversations about how much Gus was missed. In the middle of the afternoon I sat at the reading table helping a student with math. The phone rang and I reached back and picked up the receiver.

The secretary in the office said, "You have an urgent call from someone at the high school that needs to speak to you about an accident that just occurred there on the main road across from the school." My heart began to pound as I placed the phone to my ear. The caller was a former classmate of one of my sisters.

"Your sister and mom have been in a car accident in

front of the high school. An approaching car made a sudden left hand turn directly in front of them. Both your sister and mom are conscious but have been taken to the hospital."

Several members of the staff offered to drive me to the hospital but I had to check on my husband who had left for chemo treatment earlier in the day. After making quick calls to my sisters, I continued on the thirty agonizing miles to the nearest hospital.

My sister had several bruises and broken bones, but my mom had serious internal injuries and died within the hour after admission, at the age of ninety-two. Minutes ticked away and so did the life of my mom.

But within those final minutes, we were able to embrace our mother and tell her we loved her.

"Good-bye, mom," we cried.

Then, my sisters and I sat on the edge of the bed and spontaneously sang "Jesus Loves Me" and "The Lord's Prayer." As we listened to her take her last breath, she peacefully slipped away.

I thought back to the conversation I had the day before with my students about death. Little did I know how my words to the heartbroken students would echo inside my swirling mind.

After a difficult week off from teaching while planning and attending mom's funeral, I returned to the classroom. The outpouring of love and support from staff, parents, students, and community members helped sustain me through a very difficult time in my life. Returning to the daily routine of teaching helped bring some needed structure and refocusing. Experiencing the deaths of our guinea pig and my mom together helped strengthen the already strong bond between students and teacher.

Throughout my years of teaching some of the most difficult challenges were helping a child through a terminal illness or sudden loss of his or her parent. Unfortunately, there have been several instances. A young mother had been battling cancer for several years. She and her husband met with me at the beginning of a new school year to discuss how her treatments and failing health might affect their young son's performance and behavior in school. I talked with the family often and they kept me up to date on the progression of the disease through notes and phone calls. The news was not good as the young mother's condition deteriorated as the school year advanced.

Finally, as the end seemed near, a decision was made to allow their young son to remain at home with his dying mom and relatives who had gathered. Days turned into weeks. After many conversations, the family decided that the little boy should return to school.

In the middle of the morning of his first day back to school, the curly haired boy walked up to me where I was sitting at the reading table. He sat down in my lap and wrapped his arms around me. Then, he whispered in my ear, "My mom is going to die today, I think. It's time."

I choked back the tears as I pulled him close to me.

He got up and returned to his seat to eat his snack.

A few minutes later, the phone rang.

"She's gone." I heard the father's voice. "I'll be there shortly."

Upon dad's arrival, I shared with him his son's earlier premonition. We both felt the impact of what had happened. Somber little faces searched mine for answers as they watched their friend and classmate walk out of the room in the arms of his dad.

"Did she die, Mrs. S? Did his mom really die? Can we make him cards?"

"I hope my mom doesn't die. I feel so bad."

The tragedies of life often smack hard in the middle of an ordinary day. They hit you with pain and undeniable reassessment of all that is really important in life. My students and I bonded ever deeply through sharing and grieving together.

Whether you're a parent, a beginning or veteran teacher, you are never prepared for that moment when your heart aches for a child. You do what you can to comfort and support the child in any way possible.

During the long five years that my late husband struggled with lung cancer, I continued to teach, taking occasional leaves of absences during periods of crisis and setbacks. Although the structure and distractions provided by the classroom environment helped me stay grounded, I know it did not provide my students with the ideal learning environment for many of those stressful times. I'll be forever grateful to my long-term substitute teacher, colleagues, administrators, family, friends and parents for providing me with the support, guidance, and strength to get through some very challenging times following his death.

I was so glad to have my students near me. They lifted my spirits with their funny accounts and observations. My life changed overnight but these youngsters counted on me to carry on. I would get through this. You fall down. You get up. They helped to take the loneliness away.

It's okay to cry.

Chapter Nineteen
The Snake

The train was bearing down. I could hear the whistle echoing through the town as the big silver engine came into sight. I waited with the kindergarten students at the station platform. Teachers and students were so excited to be riding the Sunday River Express on a special field trip to celebrate passenger rail service in our town, after an absence of many years. As we waited, I kept a watchful eye on a couple of very active children.

Suddenly, one little blond-haired boy bounded from the group and headed for the tracks.

My heart pounded as I leaped forward, trying to run as fast as I could to fetch him, however, I found that my feet were frozen in place. My shoes of concrete prevented me from moving. I was horrified at the sight. I tried to scream but only a gasp of air spouted forth. Over and over I attempted to shout and scream to no avail.

I screamed over and over, "Stop. Stop. No. No."

My own terrifying screams aloud caused me to awake from my nightmare on the train tracks.

I heard my husband calling my name in alarm, "Norma, are you all right? You must have had a bad dream."

"I don't think I want to go on this field trip today after the bad dream I just had."

Upon arrival at school that morning I recalled the horrifying details of the dream to my teaching colleagues. I relayed my trepidation surrounding the impending trip. As a result, I had a little partner on that trip. The blond-haired boy and I shared a seat and he never left my side during the entire expedition. The journey was a great learning experience, for most of the children had never before ridden on a train. That night I slept soundly.

Recently in a television interview I overheard the former Commissioner of Education for the State of Maine. He mentioned that he had dreams about school during his years of teaching in the classroom. I thought to myself, now he's been in the trenches. He knows that our students and the responsibilities of being in charge of their safety is carried with us night and day. My worst fear was having something happen to one of my students under my care, whether we were on a field trip, on the playground, or in the classroom.

In another dream, I had forgotten where I had parked my car. Now many of us have done this in real life. I lost my car once at the mall on a very foggy night. From every mall exit the scene was the same—white-out and no cars in sight. I ended up cruising around with a security guard until we located it. My car was exactly where I had parked it.

Anyway, in this dream, I went into a big indoor flea market to get help. But I was unable to get back out. There were all these dark hallways filled with junk. (I think I watched too many episodes of American Pickers.) For hours I wandered around the collections of old tin signs, hanging lamps, rusty garden tools and large trunks, trying to find an exit. As I crawled through the cobwebs I finally spotted the red exit sign beyond the old bins of nails.

As I stepped forward to squeeze through the passageway, a large green snake uncoiled from his nest on a tattered burlap grain sack covering the nail bin. As he raised his head, he stuck out his long red tongue and hissed. Then, as I attempted to pass by, he bit me. I felt that bite on my arm in my dream. Startled, I awoke. As I dressed for school, I wondered why I had dreamed about a snake. I had not seen any. Or had I?

Later that morning, as I was placing the corrected math papers in the student mailboxes, I saw the snake. It was in my hand. The snake was a clip art design on the bottom of the math page.

The student had colored it bright green with a long red tongue. That image must have stuck in my brain when I corrected the math facts.

I thought when my teaching days came to an end, so too would the endless nights of crazy dreams about kids and the classroom. That is not the case at all. Those dreams continue to this day, years later. The bad dreams have diminished, but when I least expect it, I find myself tossing and turning trying to resolve a classroom trauma. There is one recurring dream. I've dreamed the same dream over and over. I'm trying to link it to an over indulgence in chocolate, perhaps.

It is August 31st. In our small town in Maine, it is the first day of school. I arrive on the first day in my jeans and sweatshirt. The room is full of unpacked boxes of supplies. I lift my head to gaze around the classroom. Oh, no. I realize that the classroom is packed with parents and about twenty-five boys and girls. What if our principal came in to check on our first day? He did not approve of teachers wearing jeans and sweatshirts, only if we were going on a field trip to a farm. I had arrived to set up my classroom in advance of the first day only to discover that I was not prepared. Somehow I had misplaced the first day. My room was not set up. No lessons were written in the plan book. Students were sprawled all over the floor in different groups. They had pulled out every game, book, toy, and were tossing them around. Kids were yelling and shouting at each other. It was complete chaos. Deciding to make the best of a bad situation, I attempted to maintain order and bring the classroom under control. The children ignored me. After all, no words were coming out of my open mouth. Students grew more and more unruly. I tried to take hot lunch and milk counts and there was no paper.

Tossing and turning, I wrestled with myself over how this calamity could happen. Then it was time for busses and I had no idea who was supposed to go on which busses.

Parents were yelling and shouting at each other all trying to give orders. I felt embarrassed. I felt unprepared. I felt humiliated. I felt frustrated and incompetent. How could this be happening?

I felt a soft touch on my cheek. I awoke to my big coon cat purring, asking to crawl under the covers. What a relief. The irony is that I always would set up my room at least two weeks in advance of opening day. I enjoyed dressing professionally and felt it important for teachers to dress appropriately. Classroom management and discipline were areas in which I took pride in establishing and felt comfortably in charge of my teaching responsibilities. So, why do I keep having these recurring dreams of ineffectiveness? Hmmm. What are these dreams trying to tell me I wonder?

So, teachers, if you think you'll retire and leave the classroom behind you, beware the nights of teacher dreams. When your life for over thirty years spins around the cosmos of kids, some of those worldly memories don't instantly fade.

Words from the past can float around and appear in dreamy pieces of paper in kid handwriting.

"I will not stick out my tongue or be rude."

"I love my teacher."

"I don't like my teacher. She annoys me."

But, the greatest words that linger are, "I get it. I get it now."

"I love to read."

"Can I write all the time?"

They were just kids, those students of mine. But those kids filled my life with love and understanding, constantly awakening me to the simple truths about ourselves and our often complicated world.

Chapter Twenty
The Last Hug

Standing on the curb at the end of the bus turn-around driveway, the entire school staff waited for the students to load the busses for the journey home and the start of summer vacation. This last day ritual on a hot June day had become an annual tradition to bid farewell to students. After all the excited youngsters were seated, the long yellow busses began to roll, with horns toot-tooting, and children waving arms wildly filled with anticipation of carefree days ahead.

"Good-bye, good-bye."

As the one remaining bus made the gradual turn to pass by us, I watched to see if I could catch the eyes of one of my students for the last time. This little girl with tangled hair came to me on the first day of school in September, wide-eyed, full of energy and often angry outbursts of defiant behavior. Throughout the year, this thin, lanky bundle of spirit would consume much of my energy while I attempted to help her learn some self-control and progress in academics. But, at the end of every day, she would run back from the dismissal line to give me one last hug.

She held a strong often negative opinion about a few of her peers and was impatient with their habits and comments. These pronouncements caused a few classroom disruptions and friction. Her aggressive punctuated remarks and body language didn't exactly bring out the best responses from the other students. Consequently, the whole class and I spent a great deal of time working on what it means to be respectful and tolerant of others. But at the end of every day, she would run back from the dismissal line to give me one last hug.

She seemed to have a love/hate relationship with another strong-willed classmate, a little boy.

"Why are you so mean?" He asked her one day.

With her hands on her hips and her head leaned forward, she faced her little oppositions with a sparkle in her eyes and a blustering voice of disapproval.

"Because I'm from Massachusetts." she expounded.

"No you're not," he replied. "You are from Maine."

However, in these confrontations, there was a hint that something else was developing under all this noise. I sensed a softening, a growing acceptance by each other that perhaps they were beginning to understand and harmonize their differences. As the weeks turned into months, the students formed a bond of acceptance. I had witnessed a few small miracles this school year. At the end of every day, she would run back from her place in dismissal line to give me one last hug and something else… hugs for many of her surprised classmates.

As the last line of students boarded the bus that day, she ran back to give me one last hug, crying loudly as the tears stained my blouse. As she turned to climb the steps into the bus, I heard her sobs increase to loud sad wails. As I walked to the curb to join the rest of the staff walking to our farewell spot, I wondered how her summer would be without her school family at her side.

The sound of the bus engine and loud toot caused me to strain to find the face of this cherub.

And there it was. With her face and nose pressed up against the window pane, big wet tears streamed down her face, her mouth opened sobbing uncontrollably, her cries audible through the open window. She raised both her hands over her head and moved her lips, "I'll miss you."

Tears filled my eyes and emotions stirred deep within my heart.

Every year on the last day of school as the last bus pulled away with precious children whose lives have enriched mine, my thoughts always returned to that place years ago that reaffirmed why it is I chose to be a teacher. However, in return, I learned invaluable lessons from my students.

One of our favorite classroom science activities was to peer through a large magnifying glass at snowflakes. We'd usually go outside to catch them on our parkas during the beginning of a storm when the flakes were big and fluffy.

The students were thrilled to discover that each snowflake was unique and different, even though it contained six points. As we were lining up to come inside, one of the students summed up the lesson with words of wisdom, "The snowflakes are just like us, we're all different, too."

Valuable Lessons For Life

1. Look up often for dinosaurs in the sky.

2. Celebrate the best in nature with shouts of, "Ain't this just awesome." Better yet, use proper grammar and shout, "Wow, how awesome." After all, a teacher is the author and I need to set a good example.

3. Check all your work.

4. Don't be afraid to make a mistake.

5. Always screw down the cap.

6. Play Giant Steps and Red Light.

7. Make mud pies and decorate with daisy petals.

8. Throw your "uglies" into the garbage.

9. Close the door to the bathroom and sing loudly.

10. Talk to yourself a lot cause it will make you feel not lonely.

11. Look before you sit.

12. Don't walk backwards down Main Street.
13. Keep a "red button" on the floor for emergencies.
14. Beware of humming or you might lose your memory.
15. Write. Sing. Act.
16. Sing "America the Beautiful."
17. Run back to give one last hug.
18. Keep duct tape in your drawer.
19. It's okay to cry.
20. Give attention when someone is "being good."

Glossary of Educational Terms & Acronyms

This is by no means a comprehensive list, but is provided as an introduction to the terms and acronyms that school teachers and administrators might use and parents may or may not understand. For other terms and definitions check with your favorite teacher. She (or he) will be glad to help.

At Risk Students. If students are not successful in school based upon test scores, attendance, or behavior problems, they may be identified as "at risk."

Benchmarks. Academic goals expected of students at each developmental level, age, or grade.

BIP. Behavior Intervention Plan

Charter Schools. Publicly founded schools that are run by groups of teachers, parents, or foundations.

Differentiated Instruction. The use of different types of teaching methods designed to meet individual needs of students.

DRA or Developmental Reading Assessment. This standardized reading test is used to determine a student's instructional level in reading.

ESL or English as a Second Language.

Fine Motor. Functions that require tiny muscle movement such as writing or typing.

Gross Motor. Functions that require use of large muscle movements such as walking or jumping.

GT or Gifted and Talented.

Heterogeneous Grouping. A practice that places students of different ability levels together for classroom instruction.

Homogeneous Grouping. A practice that places students of like ability levels together for classroom instruction.

IEP or Individualized Educational Plan. A written legal document that states an intervention strategy for special needs children.

LEP or Limited English Proficency.

Looping. A practice where the teacher moves with his or her students to the next grade level, rather than sending students to another teacher the next school year.

NCLB or No Child Left Behind. A federal law that requires yearly student testing, requires all teachers to be highly qualified, and provides consequences for schools not meeting standards.

NECAP or New England Common Assessment Program. A yearly assessment used by certain states to meet

NCLB requirements for testing in reading/math.

ODD or Oppositional Defiant Disorder. Children who display defiant or anti-social behaviors.

OT or Occupational Therapy. A school-based program designed to assist students with being more successful in their daily school activities or "occupations" such as handwriting, organization, social skills, behaviors.

Rubric. A scoring guide that lists what work students must show to be proficient.

Standards. Descriptions of what students should know and be able to do in required academic subjects at each grade level.

CPSIA information can be obtained
at www.ICGtesting.com
Printed in the USA
FSHW021132260619
59377FS

9 781934 949719